GLASGOW,
CLYDESIDE
AND
STIRLING

FOREWORD

Twentieth-century Scotland has a heritage of human endeavour stretching back some ten thousand years, and a wide range of man-made monuments survives as proof of that endeavour. The rugged character of much of the Scottish landscape has helped to preserve many antiquities which elsewhere have vanished beneath modern development or intensive deep ploughing, though with some 10,200 km of coastline there has also been an immeasurable loss of archaeological sites as a result of marine erosion. Above all, perhaps, the preservation of such a wide range of monuments should be credited to Scotland's abundant reserves of good building stone, allowing not only the creation of extraordinarily enduring prehistoric houses and tombs but also the development of such remarkable Scottish specialities as the medieval tower-house and the iron-age broch. This volume is one of a series of eight handbooks which have been designed to provide up-to-date and authoritative introductions to the rich archaeological heritage of the various regions of Scotland, highlighting the most interesting and best preserved of the surviving monuments and setting them in their original social context. The time-scale is the widest possible, from relics of World War II or the legacy of 19th century industrial booms back through history and prehistory to the earliest pioneer days of human settlement, but the emphasis varies from region to region, matching the particular directions in which each has developed. Some monuments are still functioning (lighthouses for instance), others are still occupied as homes, and many have been taken into the care of the State or the National Trust for Scotland, but each has been chosen as specially deserving a visit.

Thanks to the recent growth of popular interest in these topics, there is an increasing demand for knowledge to be presented in a readily digestible form and at a moderate price. In sponsoring this series, therefore, the Royal Commission on the Ancient and Historical Monuments of Scotland broadens the range of its publications with the aim of making authentic information about the man-made heritage available to as wide an audience as possible. This is the second edition of the series, in which more monuments, museums and visitor centres have been added in order to reflect the way in which the management and presentation of Scotland's past have expanded over the last decade. The excursions section proved very popular and has been both expanded and illustrated in colour.

The author, Jack Stevenson, has not only pursued his fieldwork interests as an Investigator with the Royal Commission on the Ancient and Historical Monuments of Scotland over the past twenty-one years, but he was previously engaged on a specific study of the relationships between monuments and their landscape in Central Region. As co-founder and co-editor of the *Scottish Archaeological Review*, he is closely involved with the current development of Scottish archaeology.

Monuments have been grouped according to their character and date and, although only the finest, most interesting or best preserved have been described in detail, attention has also been drawn to other sites worth visiting in the vicinity. Each section has its own explanatory introduction, beginning with the most recent monuments and gradually retreating in time back to the earliest traces of prehistoric man.

Each major monument is numbered and identified by its district so that it may easily be located on the end-map, but it is recommended that the visitor should also use the relevant 1:50,000 maps published by the Ordnance Survey as its Landranger Series, particularly for the more remote sites. Sheet nos 51, 57, 58 and 65 cover the Forth Valley and Stirling; Glasgow, Renfrew and Ayr are on sheets 63, 64, 70, 76 and 77, while the monuments in the Upper Clyde Valley appear on sheet 72. The National Grid Reference for each site is provided (eg NS 881923) as well as local directions at the head of each entry.

An asterisk (*) indicates that the site is subject to restricted hours of opening; unless attributed to Historic Scotland or the National Trust for Scotland (NTS), the visitor should assume the monument to be in private ownership and **should seek permission locally to view it**. It is of course vital that visitors to any monument should observe the country code and take special care to fasten gates. Where a church is locked, it is often possible to obtain the key from the local manse, post office or general store.

We have made an attempt to estimate how accessible each monument may be for disabled visitors, indicated at the head of each entry by a wheelchair logo and a number: 1=easy access for all visitors, including those in wheelchairs; 2=reasonable access for pedestrians but restricted access for wheelchairs; 3=restricted access for all disabled but a good view from the road or parking area; 4=access for the able-bodied only.

Many of the sites mentioned in this handbook are held in trust for the nation by the Secretary of State for Scotland and cared for on his behalf by Historic Scotland. Further information about these monuments, including details of guide-books to individual properties, can be obtained from Historic Scotland, Longmore House, Salisbury Place, Edinburgh EH9 1SH. Information about properties in the care of the National Trust for Scotland can be obtained from the National Trust for Scotland, 5 Charlotte Square, Edinburgh EH2 4DU.

ANNA RITCHIE
Series Editor

ACKNOWLEDGEMENTS

Many of the entries in this volume are based on material prepared for inclusion either in the Royal Commission on the Ancient and Historical Monuments of Scotland's Inventories or in the Archaeological Sites and Monuments Series, and I am therefore indebted to many present and former colleagues for the fruits of their original research. In particular I would like to record my gratitude to Dr J N G Ritchie, Mr P Corser, Mr S P Halliday, Mr R J C Mowat, Mr G P Stell and Mr G S Maxwell for their support and assistance. The volume also owes much to the work, over many years, of the Commission's photographic and drawing staff under Mr G B Quick and Mr I G Scott respectively, and to the efforts of Mr J Keggie, who photographed several of the sites at short notice.

Under Miss C H Cruft, and more recently Dr J N G Ritchie, the staff of the National Monuments Record of Scotland, particularly Mr K McLaren and Mrs R Wimberley, helped with information on various buildings and provided numerous photographs and drawings. Miss S Learmonth typed the manuscript. Mr J White, Historic Scotland, was very helpful in providing photographs.

I am grateful to Mr J G Dunbar for reading the medieval sections of the volume; finally I am indebted to my patient editor, Dr A Ritchie, for her encouragement and assistance throughout the preparation of this book.

The majority of the photographs are the work of the Commission's Photographic Department or are from the Photographic Library of Historic Scotland or are from the National Monuments Record of Scotland, and these are Crown Copyright. Author and publisher are gratefully indebted to the following institutions and individuals for permission to publish photographs and plans: Historic Scotland (pp. 26, 27, 35, 38, 39, 41, 42, 43, 44, 46, 47, 51, 79, 80 bottom, 82 top, 85, 86, 89, 90 bottom, 94 top, 95, 96 bottom, 97, 109 top, 110, 111, 112, 113 right, 114 bottom, 116, 118, 119 bottom, 120, 125, 127, 131 bottom, 133 top, 134 top, 136, 137, 148, 151, 157, 160, 161, 162); the National Trust for Scotland (pp. 29, 31, 32, 33, 34, 36 top, 48 bottom, 59 left, 69, 71, 73 bottom, 74, 75, 76, 77, 78 top, 81); Royal Museum of Scotland (pp. 123, 124); Mansell Collection (p. 55); G Cobb (p. 60 left); P Corser (p. 104); T E Gray (p. 109 right).

Biggar Gas Works

INTRODUCTION

Continuity and change in the landscape: motte, tower-house and modern farm steading at Carleton, South Ayrshire

The area included within this volume straddles central Scotland from the Firth of Clyde to the North Sea, and extends from the Grampian Highlands to the Southern Uplands. Thus, although it embraces much of what is often referred to as Lowland Scotland, it is in fact made up of a number of discrete landscapes ranging from low-lying carseland to subalpine mountain. Each of these varying landscapes has had a distinctive effect on the development of human settlement from the earliest times to the present day, and this has resulted in an area which is rich in monuments of most periods and which contains a variety of remains not surpassed elsewhere in Scotland.

The Forth-Clyde isthmus, which lies at the heart of the region, has traditionally been one of the major geographical divides in Scotland, separating east from west and north from south. The importance of this line has been recognised since the 1st century AD when Tacitus, the biographer of Agricola (the Governor of Roman Britain and conqueror of southern Scotland), commented on the marked racial and tribal differences to be seen on either side of the Forth. The reasons for these differences were probably partly determined by the terrain, as until the 18th century the low-lying valley of the Forth was blanketed by extensive peat-mosses, which acted as a more effective barrier to communication than would a corresponding area of open water. Immediately north of the Forth lie stretches of gently rolling country which on the east are bounded by the steep north face of the Ochils and on the west by the Highland Massif.

To the south of the Forth the Gargunnock Hills, Campsie Fells and Kilpatrick Hills extend the north-east/south-west trend of the Ochils, and act as a further hindrance to north-south communication. South of these volcanic hills, the country opens out to the valleys of the Kelvin and Clyde, which rest on sedimentary strata of Carboniferous age containing large deposits of coal, iron ore and limestone. The exploitation of these deposits, which extend to the south-west of the Clyde to Ayrshire, provided the basis for the 19th century industrial boom followed by an inevitable decline, as the deposits were exhausted. The upper stretches of the Clyde, however, reach beyond the confines of the Midland Valley, and across the Southern Upland Fault near Abington, to rise in the hills of the Southern Uplands close to the Dumfries border. To the west of the Clyde, and again ringed by hills which isolate the area from the outside, are the Ayrshire lowlands, spreading from Ballantrae in the south to the hills of Renfrew in the north. Finally, situated in the Firth of Clyde there is the Isle of Arran; its geology and scenery would place it in Argyll, but from early times it has had close ties with the east, and there are sound historical reasons for its inclusion in North Ayrshire, rather than Argyll.

The seven principal regions covered by this volume—the Highlands, the Forth Valley, the Central Belt, the Southern Uplands, Ayr and Renfrew, and Arran—represent the geography of Scotland in microcosm, and the wide range of physical backgrounds to the various areas has played an influential part in determining both the types of monuments that were originally built and those that have survived to the present day. A few examples will serve to illustrate the complex and dynamic relationship between the physical environment and the archaeological record. Arran is remarkable for the number and quality of its neolithic and bronze-age remains. This is in part a reflection of the suitability of the island for settlement during those periods, but it is also a witness to the climatic deterioration of the 1st millennium BC, which rendered much of what had hitherto been good agricultural land as marginal pasture or peat bog, thus sparing many of the monuments from the depredations of more recent agriculture. Similarly, the relatively remote area of Upper Clydesdale contains an outstanding array of late bronze-age and iron-age settlement sites which no doubt extended further down the valley of the Clyde, but they are now overwhelmed by more recent agriculture and urban development. The settlements have only survived in

Upper Clydesdale because the area has been used for sheep runs, and it is only now that these important prehistoric landscapes (as opposed to individual monuments) are threatened by large-scale land improvements and forestry plantations. The landscape is, however, never static and the process of partial replacement is always in action, and even urban areas cannot escape it. In Glasgow, parts of the 19th century industrial landscape have already been obliterated and replaced by more modern buildings, while in other sections of the city the older buildings are being carefully restored and put to new uses.

Although buildings and monuments described in this book are treated on an individual basis (reducing them to the status of highly prized museum objects), they are but one element in a constantly evolving landscape, and to gain the maximum appreciation of each site the visitor should never forget to look outwards from the particular monument to see how it fits in to its geographical and historical setting.

The Mesolithic Period (c 8000 BC–4000 BC)

The earliest human groups to occupy West Central Scotland have left few visible traces, but their activities are well attested, particularly on the raised beaches of the Ayrshire coast and along the gravel terraces of the River Clyde, by numerous flint scatters, which indicate the camp sites of these wandering hunter-gatherers. Each of the mesolithic bands may have occupied a large territory, exploiting a range of food resources in different zones at different times of the year. Along the south shore of the Forth, in the area around Grangemouth, there is a series of oyster-shell middens (sometimes visible in newly ploughed fields as white smudges) which are the refuse heaps of groups of hunter-gatherers; they were formerly all thought to be of mesolithic date, but recent excavations have shown that some, at least, are later and belong to the neolithic period.

The Neolithic Period (4000 BC–2500 BC)

At about the beginning of the fourth millennium BC (c 4000 BC), new groups of settlers began to penetrate the area. They probably worked their way up the coast from the South or from Ireland and, like their mesolithic forebears, were accomplished sailors well able to cross short stretches of open water to colonise off-shore islands such as Arran. The neolithic peoples brought two important innovations with them: the construction of large stone or timber monuments, and farming (both arable and pastoral). The development of farming was to have a dramatic impact on the environment as it not only precipitated a major population explosion but also accelerated the rate of destruction of the natural forest cover which had begun in the mesolithic period. Deforestation was in part deliberate, some areas being cleared by felling and burning (hence the importance of the archetypal neolithic tool, the stone axe), while continued browsing by domesticated animals helped to prevent forest regeneration.

Of the houses and fields of the first farmers we know little. The houses of the living appear to have been predominantly rectangular in plan and built of timber; the houses of the dead, on the other hand, were frequently more substantial and long-lasting, being either of earth or stone, and many survive as Scotland's first examples of monumental architecture. These chambered cairns were communal burial-places used for successive interments over a long period of time, and it is likely that each separate community had its own tomb. Thus, from a study of the cairns it is possible to get some idea of the distribution and location of the early farming groups. From this we can see that the distribution of the cairns is biased towards coastal and low-lying positions and, not surprisingly, they are frequently closely related to areas of modern agriculture. In some cases, however, they lie in moorland, far removed from present-day arable land, but much of what was farmland in the fourth to the first millennium BC has since been swamped by peat, which has grown partly as a result of a deterioration in the climate (wetter and cooler) and partly because of the over-exploitation and eventual exhaustion of the soil by the early farmers.

The Bronze Age (c 2500 BC to 700 BC)

The transition from the neolithic period to the bronze age is dated to about the mid-third millennium BC and is characterised by a complex series of changes in the archaeological record, which includes new forms of burial and ritual monuments, the introduction and development of new pottery styles, altered forms of settlements, and finally (and perhaps least significantly) the introduction of metal-working (firstly copper and gold, soon to be followed by bronze).

Towards the later third millennium the tradition of communal burial in chambered cairns came to an end and was replaced by a series of individual burial rites involving inhumation and cremation. The remains were normally deposited in a grave and were frequently accompanied by a pot (Beaker, Food Vessel or Cinerary Urn) or some other form of artefact. These graves often occur singly, but they were also grouped together to form small cemeteries, which in some cases were marked by the construction of a covering mound. The mounds are normally round and vary greatly in size, ranging from as little as 2 m to more than 40 m in diameter (see no. 102). The construction of the covering mound did not, however, neccessarily mark the final stage in the use of the cairn and excavation has shown that burials were often inserted into a pre-existing cairn (see no. 100).

During the bronze age the area of land that was settled expanded rapidly, and by the middle of the second millennium large parts of the country had been colonised by farming communities—possibly equalling or even surpassing the area under cultivation in the medieval period. Because of the greater number of settlements available for study, we know considerably more about the nature of bronze-age houses and farms than in the preceding neolithic period. There are good examples of dispersed farmsteads, consisting of hut-circles and stone walled fields, on the moorland around Moss Farm, Arran (no. 96). These fields are clear evidence for arable farming and this is corroborated by the discovery, during the course of excavation, of charred grain and cereal pollen.

The economic basis for the late bronze-age unenclosed settlements in Upper Clydesdale (nos 92-93) is less easy to ascertain; they are not normally associated with contemporary fields and this, taken in conjunction with their upland situation (about 300 m OD), might suggest that they were the settlements of pastoralists exploiting the grasslands of the Southern Uplands in much the same way as do the present farmers.

The Iron Age (c 700 BC–AD 400)

The spread of iron technology throughout Britain in the 7th century had little immediate impact on the mass of the population; more significant was a series of changes to the economic and social framework that began to manifest themselves at about the same period. These changes ended a phase of settlement whose origins lay in the neolithic, and they established a new order which was to survive, albeit in a much modified form, for at least a thousand years. Interrupted briefly by the Roman interlude, the iron age, or more aptly the Age of Forts, did not finally end until the Norman supremacy in the 12th century.

By the middle of the 1st millennium BC the characteristic open settlements of the bronze age were steadily being replaced by a range of defended enclosures. These were designed to deter human, not animal predators, and were probably made neccessary because the deteriorating climate had reduced the amount of agricultural land available, leading to internecine struggles to secure control over the remainder. The west, and Arran in particular, was more vulnerable than other areas to the effects of the increasingly wet and cool climate, and there the impact on population figures must have been dramatic, with the abandonment of large tracts of hitherto prime areas of farmland. Elsewhere, the settlement pattern was adjusted and many of the upland areas, such as Upper Clydesdale, continued to support sizeable populations.

The defensive sites varied greatly from one area to another; in the west small stone-walled forts and duns predominate, while in the east larger and more strongly defended forts, settlements and homesteads, which relied on vast quantities of timber for the construction of the defences, are to be found. Duns and homesteads were occupied by single families but the forts and settlements housed larger communities, and if the various types of settlement were in use contemporaneously the settlement pattern would have resembled that of today with a mixture of isolated farmsteads and small nucleated villages. Until recently little was known of the agricultural background to iron-age settlement, but in the last few years the remains of arable fields and pastoral enclosures have been found surrounding some of the sites (see no. 82), indicating that that the economy was not predominantly pastoral as had been thought previously.

In the absence of further excavation the precise dating of most of the iron-age enclosures must remain uncertain. It is clear, however, that many of the sites, particularly the forts, may have remained in use, or have been re-used, over a long period of time, but many of the larger hilltop forts in the east were probably abandoned (or at least not defended) long before the arrival of the Roman army in favour of more equable low-lying sites. Where such forts continued in use after the Roman period, their function may have altered to that of the seat of the local chief rather than that of a communal settlement.

The Roman Period (AD 80–AD 400)

The comparative isolation of iron-age Scotland was interrupted in AD 80 when Agricola, the Governor of Roman England, stormed northwards and, in four years of campaigning, established authority over that part of the country lying to the south of the Highland Line (approximately Stonehaven to Dumbarton). Control was exerted through a network of roads and forts which allowed the Roman army to contain any outbreaks of trouble. The area within Roman control was protected from the tribes to the north by a series of forts covering the mouths of the main glens leading from the Highlands. Those in west central Scotland include: Bochastle (Callander); a newly discovered site at Doune which lies on a terrace overlooking the castle (no. 35); Malling, Port of Menteith; Drumquhassle, Drymen; with the addition of Barochan which is situated on the south shore of the Clyde and protected the otherwise open westward flank. With the exception of Bochastle, all these forts have been levelled by cultivation and appear only as cropmarks.

Agricola's plan to hold the whole of lowland Scotland required large numbers of Roman troops and it strained the resources of the army. Trouble on the Continent, particularly in Germany, in the late AD 80s and 90s led to troops being withdrawn from Britain, and it was no longer possible to sustain the expansionist policy in the North. The elaborate system of forts guarding the Highland valleys was abandoned shortly after AD 86 and it is likely that most, if not all, of the forts in west central Scotland were evacuated by AD 90.

Following the retreat from Scotland, a new frontier line was eventually established across the Tyne-Solway gap, and this was consolidated in the 120s by the construction of Hadrian's Wall. With the accession of Antoninus Pius as Emperor in 138, imperial policy was reversed with Hadrian's Wall abandoned in favour of the reoccupation of southern Scotland. A static frontier was drawn across the Forth-Clyde line with a chain of forts extending northwards from a forward base at Camelon (Falkirk) into Strathearn and ending at Bertha, just north of Perth.

This complex frontier-system, of which the Antonine Wall formed the central section, comprised a series of installations (forts, smaller fortlets and signal posts) guarding the border from the Firth of Clyde in southern Renfrewshire (see nos 79 and 80) to the Firth of Forth at Inveresk, east of Edinburgh. Behind this line, the valley of the Clyde was controlled by a road linking Scotland to north-west England. Along the road (the Roman equivalent of the modern A 74), there was a line of forts and lesser installations; most of these, such as the fort at Crawford (NS 953215), have been levelled by later cultivation but the small road-post at Redshaw Burn (no. 81) can still be seen.

The early Antonine occupation of Scotland (known as Antonine I) appears to have ended in the 150s with signs of a major revolt, forcing the Roman army to abandon their forts for a short period. Reoccupation of the Wall (Antonine II), however, soon followed, but by the 160s it was again evacuated never to be re-used. The Roman army maintained a presence in southern Scotland from the late 2nd to the 4th century, but the emphasis had moved away from the west to the east, and there was no permanent garrison in west central Scotland after the abandonment of the Antonine Wall in the 160s.

The Early Historic Period (AD 400–AD 1200)

The collapse of Roman influence in Scotland was followed by major changes in the political and religious organisation of the country. On the political front, the greater part of west central Scotland was absorbed into the British-speaking kingdom of Strathclyde, whose territory included the counties of Dumbarton, Lanark, Renfrew and Ayr, and whose capital lay on the north side of the Clyde at Dumbarton Rock (no. 36). On Strathclyde's north-west frontier lay the hostile kingdom of Dalriada (roughly the equivalent of the county of Argyll), which had been in the hands of the Scotti since their arrival from Ireland sometime in the 5th century. To the northeast were the southern Picts who formed a powerful federation of the earlier iron-age tribes of eastern Scotland, and on the eastern flank Lothian was under the control of the Anglian kings of Northumbria.

During the following centuries the Scots extended their power from Dalriada to most of southern and eastern Scotland to lay the foundation for the medieval kingdom. Kenneth MacAlpin seized control of Pictland in about 843; Strathclyde fell to Malcolm II in c 1015 following a lapse in the Strathclyde royal succession, and Malcolm's victory at Carham in 1018 finally removed the Northumbrian hold on Lothian. Not all the successes, however, fell to the Scots; in the west, Viking raids and settlement established a strong Scandinavian presence along the Atlantic seaboard (possibly including Arran), which continued into the 13th century.

Christianity was introduced in the wake of the Roman occupation. The first missionary activity in west central Scotland was carried out in the early 5th century by Ninian from his base at Whithorn, Wigtownshire, from where he is reputed to have led a mission to the southern Picts. Ninian's Church was organised on an episcopal basis following the Roman tradition as was that of the later missionary, St Kentigern (or Mungo, died AD 612), whose work was closely associated with the kingdom of Strathclyde. Kentigern's seat is traditionally identified with Glasgow Cathedral (no. 54) but Govan (no. 66), with its major collection of Early Christian stones and its proximity to Dumbarton Rock, is a probable alternative. The early episcopal organisation of the Church was modified in the 7th century following the success of the Columban mission to Iona. During the next centuries monasticism, of the type associated with the Celtic Church, played an important role before it was replaced as a result of the 12th century reform of the Church. Associated with the introduction of Christianity is the growth of a vigorous tradition of stone-carving which has bequeathed to us the most tangible remains of the period in the form of a major series of decorated crosses, memorial stones and grave-markers (nos 65-68). The stone-carvers drew their inspiration from the art styles of the surrounding kingdoms, and they owed much to Irish, Pictish and Northumbrian sources; later in the period Scandinavia also played a part, even if indirectly, with the introduction of the distinctive hogback tombstones (no. 66).

The Medieval Period

The largely indigenous building traditions and ecclesiastical structure of the early historic period continued to evolve into the 12th century, but during the next two hundred years the cultural life of Scotland, for the upper echelons at least, underwent fundamental changes following the spread of Norman influences from England and the Continent. The Scottish Crown established close links with the Norman aristocracy in the South and this led to the introduction of new building styles, both military and ecclesiastical. The traditions of the Celtic Church suffered a similar fate and they were suppressed in favour of the Roman model. By the 13th century much of the country, and certainly most of west central Scotland, had been transformed into a feudal state lying on the north-west fringes of Roman Christendom. All major elements of feudalism were present, including castles, churches and towns—and the architectural history of the next four centuries is the story of the evolution of these exotic imports within a Scottish context.

As might be expected, Norman military architecture in the form of the motte-and-bailey castle heralded the arrival of the new order. Large tracts of the country were given to the new aristocracy, and at the centre of each estate a castle was built to dominate the landscape. West central Scotland is particularly well-endowed with mottes, and considerable parts of Stirlingshire, Lanarkshire and Ayrshire were made over to Norman knights (in this part of Scotland the shire system itself was largely a Norman innovation).

During the 12th and 13th centuries the Church was reorganised and brought into line with western Christendom. Its structure was based on territorial divisions, with bishops controlling dioceses from their cathedrals. West central Scotland was divided between the dioceses of Glasgow, Dunblane and St Andrews, and the medieval cathedrals of Dunblane and Glasgow are described below (nos 53 and 54). Below the level of the diocese the countryside was reorganised into a series of parishes, each provided with its own church and priest. Most of the early parish churches have been replaced by more recent buildings, but an interesting fragment remains at Lamington (no. 61), where an elaborately carved Romanesque arched doorway has been incorporated into the post-Reformation Church.

Running in parallel with the diocesan/parochial system in the Church was the other great ecclesiastical network of the middle ages—the monasteries. These were founded in considerable numbers (often on the sites of Celtic monasteries) from the early 12th century under royal or aristocratic patronage, and examples representing most of the main forms have survived the ravages of the Reformation. There is a major Cluniac abbey at Paisley (no. 59), founded by an Anglo-Norman on the site of an earlier Celtic monastery, as well as a daughter house at Crossraguel (no. 56) established by Duncan, Earl of Carrick. The Tironensians founded an important abbey at Kilwinning (no. 58) and a priory at Lesmahagow; unfortunately, the latter no longer survives as a standing building but it has recently been excavated, revealing much of its plan. The Augustinians are represented at Cambuskenneth (no. 55), where there was a large abbey, and at Inchmahome (no. 57) they established a small house beautifully situated on an island in the Lake of Menteith which, like Kilwinning, may have been sited on an earlier Celtic foundation.

In the course of the 13th century the earthwork and timber castles of the early Norman period began to be replaced by more substantial structures built of stone. In some cases an earlier site was reused, eg Dumbarton (no. 36), Stirling (no. 38), Crookston (no. 41), but in others virgin sites more appropriate to the new structures were chosen, eg Bothwell (no. 33), and Doune (no. 35). From as early as the 14th century it is possible to detect two strains in the castle building tradition that were to persist for the next three centuries, ie the division between major castles (such as Stirling, Bothwell and Dumbarton) and the more numerous hall- and tower-houses. An early example of one of the latter structures is the 13/14th-century hall-house at Lochranza, Arran (no. 43), and it is likely that this form of lightly defended house was the precursor to that peculiarly Scottish phenomenon, the tower-house, which developed in the 14th century and remained a popular form until the 18th century.

For Scotland, the 13th century was a period of comparative prosperity and peace: the fruits of Normanization were flourishing and considerable numbers of fine stone buildings were under construction. Towns, another key feature of the feudal state, were being founded along the coasts and rivers in order to encourage trade and industry, and therefore revenue, for the Crown and magnates who were the feudal superiors. This period of expansion, however, was brought to an end at the close of the century with the outbreak of the Wars of Independence against England, which were to stumble on, in one form or another, for two hundred years.

From the late 15th century the use of artillery became the dominant factor in military strategy and gradually rendered many of the existing castles obsolete. At the same time new forms of military architecture were introduced from the Continent, particularly Italy, and increasingly it was only the Crown and State that could afford or indeed were permitted to undertake such works. Sir James Hamilton of Finnart was responsible for two of the earliest artillery fortifications in Scotland: Blackness Castle (no. 32) and Craignethan Castle (no. 34); at the former an existing castle was modified, while at the latter a fresh site was chosen and a custom-built castle erected. To this period also belongs a phase of major rebuilding at Stirling Castle (no. 38) with the construction of the magnificent Palace Block for James V; elsewhere castles and tower-houses had their domestic accommodation extended, sometimes at the expense of their defensive capabilities (see nos 26, 39). In the towns the predominantly wooden domestic buildings began to be replaced in stone, and at Stirling there are particularly fine examples of Renaissance town-houses belonging to wealthy courtiers (nos 12 and 13).

The Eighteenth and Nineteenth Centuries

The Act of Union (1707) is a convenient watershed dividing medieval from post-medieval Scotland and, although many of the developments that were to transform the country over the next one hundred and fifty years had their origins in the preceding century, the political and economic climate that prevailed under the new regime had a profound effect in hastening the processes of change. Agricultural improvements, industrialisation, urban development and population growth all combined to alter the face of Scotland, and west central Scotland lay at the heart of these developments.

Agricultural improvements had a major impact on the landscape and on the lives of all those involved in it, from peasant to landlord. The land was drained and enclosed, new crops introduced and, most important of all, the old short-term tenancy agreements were replaced by longer lettings that encouraged the farmers to carry out long-term improvements to the land and buildings. Consequently, it is from this period that we have the first surviving examples of rural vernacular architecture, albeit in small numbers (nos 19 and 21). Before that date, the houses were of such poor quality that they needed to be replaced every few years. New crops and land reclamation meant greater rental income for the landlord, and it was often the landlord who led the way by introducing the new methods at the home farm (see no. 25).

A proportion of the landlords' newly acquired wealth was used to build grand mansions at the centre of the estates and Culzean (no. 25) is a prime example of this process in action. Originally it had been a simple late medieval tower-house which, in the course of the 18th century, was transformed into one of Scotland's greatest houses by one of Scotland's greatest architects, Robert Adam. But it is misleading to look only at the house, for it lay at the centre of a large, carefully contrived landscape of formal and wild gardens which separated it both physically and psychologically from the ruder world outside. Nor was Adam's work confined to the house itself; he designed the circular steading for the Home Farm which has been converted for use as a Visitor Centre. Another member of the Adam family, William, was responsible for the magnificent garden house (no. 29) in the policies of Hamilton Palace, which has been restored and opened to the public.

If the improved agricultural estate was a symbol of the 18th century then the sporting estate, as exemplified by Brodick Castle (no. 24), must represent the 19th century. Such estates were heavily dependent on outside money for their maintenance and in the period of their decline it has become fashionable to decry the efforts and aims of their builders. The great houses themselves are sometimes of dubious architectural merit, but much money was also spent on the houses of the estate workers, raising their standard of living and providing good quality accommodation which survives to this day as conspicuous features of the landscape.

Urban growth and industrialisation went hand in hand, beginning in the late 18th century after the loss of the American colonies reorientated trading patterns. Spinning and weaving were amongst the first industries to expand, followed in the 19th century by coal and iron-ore mining, heavy engineering and ship-building. Glasgow and the surrounding area was ideally suited for these developments as there were abundant local supplies of coal, iron and limestone, as well as adequate water-power. For a while, the water-powered mills at New Lanark (no. 7) formed the largest group of mills for spinning cotton and yarn in the country. Major cloth-weaving industries grew up in Renfrewshire, around Paisley, but, as late as the beginning of this century, much of the preparation of the cloth was still carried on by outworkers in the surrounding villages, and we are fortunate that one of these weavers' cottages has been preserved at Kilbarchan (no. 23).

Apart from their spoil-tips little now survives of the early extractive industries (but see no. 6) and only one example of 19th century coal-mining machinery has been preserved (no. 4). The memorials of the Victorian and Edwardian coal and iron industry are, however, fossilised in the magnificent cast-iron street furniture that still graces most the towns of west central Scotland. The traditional ship-building areas along the Clyde are now in sad decline but the flavour of their former glory can still be sampled in Govan, Port Glasgow and Greenock. Associated with the development of trade and industry was the rapid improvement in the transport system. Access to Glasgow was eased by dredging the Clyde and passage up these waters was made safer by the provision of lighthouses such as The Cloch (no. 3). East to west communication was vital, and a canal linking the Clyde to the Forth was proposed from as early as the 17th century, but was not implemented until late in the following century (no. 5). The Forth and Clyde canal soon faced competition from the railways, which themselves have been largely eclipsed by the motorway (M 8).

**Clackmannan
Stone, Tolbooth
and Mercat Cross**

EXCURSIONS

The excursions are intended to act as an introduction to a selection of the monuments described in the text. In some cases the excursions cover monuments of all ages and types while in others a specific period or theme has been selected. Besides the monuments included in the text, the opportunity has been taken to draw attention to other sites which can be seen in passing and most are easy to identify as they are marked on the relevant Ordnance Survey 1:50,000 map.

THE ANTONINE WALL

There is so much to see along the line of the Wall that it has been divided into two excursions—one looking at the eastern section and the other the western. For both excursions the Ordnance Survey 2½ inch Antonine Wall Map is an invaluable addition to the relevant 1:50,000 map; both show additional sections of the Wall which can be visited if time allows.

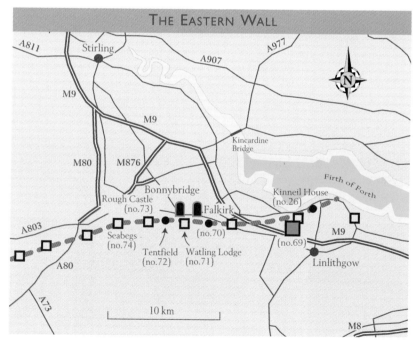

KEY	
Battle	✗
Bridge	⌒
Broch, dun, fort	O
Castle	⌑
Church	✛
Harbour	⚓
House, rural building	■
Industrial Monument	▮
Lighthouse	⌘
Long Cairn	⌇
Military Monument	�
Miscellaneous prehistoric	⦙
Monument	●
Pictish Stone	ⲓ
Roman Monument	☐
Round Cairn	☀
Standing Stone	▲
Stone Circle	○
Town, village	●
Town *explored in text*	◉

Begin at Kinneil House (no. 26), where there is a collection of Roman material in the museum attached to the house, and walk to the reconstructed fortlet (no. 69). Then take the A904 and B904 to Falkirk; between the junction of the two roads and the crossing of the River Avon, there are a number of neolithic middens composed of oyster shells which, after ploughing, show up in the fields to the left of the road as large white smudges. On the east side of Falkirk the Wall can be seen in Callendar Park (no. 70).

Kinneil House

Follow the A803 through Falkirk to the flight of locks on the Forth and Clyde Canal (no. 5) at the west end of the town (NS 875804), then turn left to the B816 and follow the Historic Scotland signs to the Antonine Wall at Watling Lodge (no. 71) and Tentfield (no. 72).

Continue along the B816 towards Bonnybridge and follow the Historic Scotland signposts to the fort at Rough Castle (no. 73), which incorporates one of the best sections of the Wall and includes a well-preserved prehistoric field-system.

Return to Bonnybridge and, before turning westwards to run along the south side of the Forth and Clyde Canal, look at the canal bridge and the Bonnybridge Iron Foundry with its eye-catching mural painting (NS 824800). About 1 km west of Bonnybridge there is a section of the Wall preserved in Seabegs Wood (no. 74) which includes one of the best surviving stretches of the Military Way.

Bearsden, Roman fort, bath-house

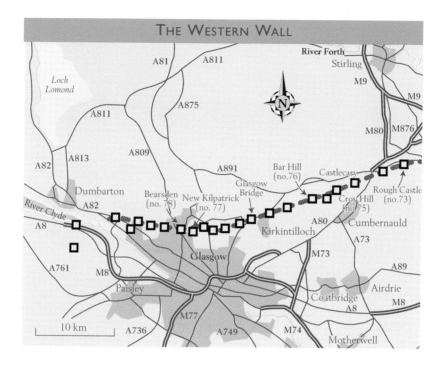

THE WESTERN WALL

Although the Antonine Wall ends some way to the west, this excursion begins in Bearsden. The fort (no. 78) was excavated in advance of house building in the 1980s but the developers, assisted by Historic Scotland, have laid out the bath block for public display. A short distance to the east of Bearsden there are two lengths of the stone plinth, on which the turf rampart was founded, exposed in New Kilpatrick Cemetery (no. 77).

After New Kilpatrick head for Kirkintilloch on the B8049, A807 and A803. From the roundabout at the junction of the A807 and A803 look out for the ditch of the Wall in the fields to the north of the road and, after crossing Glasgow Bridge over the Forth and Clyde Canal (no. 5), it can be seen on the south side of the road (the slight sag of the ditch is particularly noticeable where it is crossed by a wall or fence). Instead of turning right into the town centre, continue along the main road and turn right along the B8023 which flanks the Forth and Clyde Canal. Take a right turn into Twechar and follow the Historic Scotland signposts to the fort on Bar Hill (no. 76). On the crest of the hill to the east of the bath-house there are the much-reduced remains of an iron-age fort.

After the Bar Hill return northwards to rejoin the B8023, follow the Forth and Clyde Canal eastwards, and turn right over the canal into the village of Croy. From here the Historic Scotland signs point to one of the best stretches of the Wall with impressive lengths of rock-cut ditch (no. 75).

For those wishing to continue, additional stretches of the Wall can be seen south of Banknock and west of Castlecary (NS 778779).

Bar Hill, Roman fort, bath-house

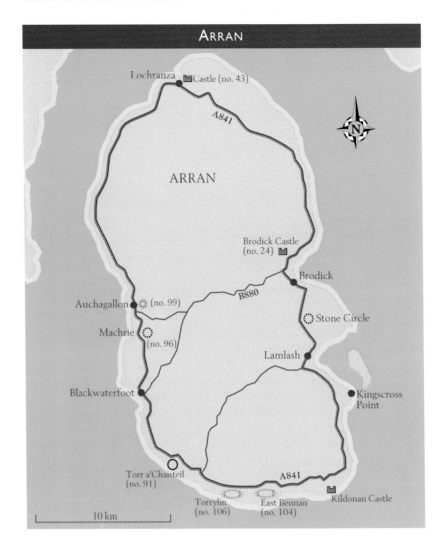

ARRAN

Lochranza
Castle (no. 43)
A841
ARRAN
Brodick Castle (no. 24)
Brodick
Auchagallon (no. 99)
B880
Stone Circle
Machrie (no. 96)
Lamlash
Blackwaterfoot
Kingscross Point
Torr a'Chaisteil (no. 91)
A841
Torrylin (no. 106)
East Bennan (no. 104)
Kildonan Castle
10 km

The Arran excursion is designed to take the visitor on a trip around the island in order to see as much of the magnificent scenery and as wide a range of monuments as possible. Those with less than a full day to spare may wish either to visit Brodick Castle on another day or to omit the section around the north end and go directly from Brodick, via The String Road, to Auchagallon.

From Brodick follow the main island road (A 841) northwards to Brodick Castle (no. 24), passing the Arran Museum on the right at NS 011373. After the castle continue northwards to Lochranza Castle (no. 43), then on around the north-west coast to the cairn at Auchagallon (no. 99). Those who would enjoy the exercise can visit the island's most impressive prehistoric monuments at Moss Farm, Machrie (no. 96), otherwise pass through Blackwaterfoot and, at Corriecravie, walk out to the iron-age dun at Torr a' Chaisteil (no. 91). Then go on to the chambered cairn at Torrylin (no. 106).

If time permits, there is another well-preserved neolithic cairn at East Bennan (no. 104). Thereafter the A 841 continues round the coast where slight diversions lead to Kildonan Castle (NS 037210), and a dun at Kingscross Point (NS 056283). Finally, immediately east of the main road and by a conveniently sited lay-by at the highest point on the road between Lamlash and Brodick, there is a small stone circle (NS 018336).

Brodick Castle

AYRSHIRE

The rich Ayrshire lowlands contain a wealth of monuments, particularly those dating to the medieval and later periods. Two of the following excursions look at groups of sites in the north and south of the former county, while the third visits buildings associated with Robert Burns. All three are well-suited to visitors staying in, or around, Ayr.

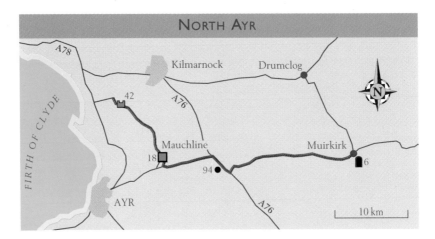

This excursion begins in Muirkirk (no. 6), home of the Scottish coal and iron industry, where there are the fascinating remains of old coal and iron workings, as well as the foundations of 'Tar' MacAdam's original tar works. Although this is some distance from the other sites in this trip, it offers the opportunity to see some of the best-preserved remains of early industry which are rapidly being swept away by open-cast mining and land reclamation schemes.

From Muirkirk head for the cup-and-ring markings at Ballochmyle (no. 94) by turning westwards for Sorn on the A 70 and B 743, then through Catrine on the B 713 to the A 76. Turn right towards Mauchline and take the minor road to the site.

From Ballochmyle rejoin the A 76 and turn on to the A 758 in Mauchline (where there is a small museum) and follow the signs for Tarbolton. In the centre of the town, which has strong associations with Burns, there is the Bachelors Club (no. 18), and, on the outskirts of the town along the B 744, the remains of a motte-and-bailey castle.

Built on a rather grander scale than the motte at Tarbolton is the castle at Dundonald (no. 42), which lies to the north-west on the B 730. Dundonald was the favourite haunt of the early Stewart kings and has recently been partially excavated.

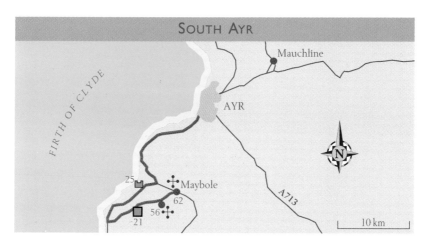

SOUTH AYR

This excursion takes in a group of sites to the south of the town of Ayr. It includes a visit to the house and country park of Culzean, which could easily occupy a whole day itself.

Culzean Castle

Detail of oval staircase in Culzean Castle

From Ayr follow the coast road (A 719) to Dunure, and take a short detour into the village to see the medieval castle and its later dovecot. Continue south on the A 719, up Electric Brae, where an optical illusion gives the impression that the road descends rather than climbs the hill, until the signposted entrance to Culzean Country Park (no. 25) is reached.

After Culzean turn southwards and pass through the village of Maidens towards Turnberry. Before reaching the village, Turnberry lighthouse and its adjacent ruined medieval castle can be seen across the famous golf course. In Turnberry join the A 77 and head north-eastwards for Crossraguel Abbey and Maybole.

The A 77 leads through Kirkoswald and passes Souter Johnnie's House (no. 21) on the right and the former parish church on the left. Crossraguel Abbey (no. 56) lies about 3 km north-east of Kirkoswald. Finally, in Maybole there are the remains of a collegiate church (no. 62) and a fine tower-house which occupies a prominent position in the centre of the town.

BURNS TOUR

Beginning in the centre of Ayr take the Alloway Road (B 7024) which leads directly to Burn's Cottage (no. 19) on the north side of the town. Then drive into the centre of Alloway; on the left is the Burn's Heritage Centre and a short step further on to the right there are the remains of the Old Kirk of Alloway. The earliest portions of the church may date from the 13th century but it has been heavily modified and includes much later work. There is a 17th-century belfry and a medieval gravestone has been used to form the lintel for a window in the south wall. After the church the road divides; on the left is the Burn's Memorial and, between it and the hotel, the old road leads down to the Old Brig o'Doon. This was built in the 15th century and restored in 1832.

Continue along the B 7024 and from Maybole take the A 77 to Kirkoswald. On the left hand side of the street stands Souter Johnnie's House (no. 21) and a little further on to the right are the remains of the old parish church set in its graveyard wherein lie several of the characters made famous in Burns' poems: Hugh Rodger, Douglas Graham and John Davidson (Tam O'Shanter). The church has been heavily restored but is probably medieval in origin.

Another building associated with Burns, the Bachelors' Club (no. 18), lies in Tarbolton on the north-east side of Ayr. It is included in the North Ayr excursion but can be reached with ease from Kirkoswald by returning past Ayr on the A 77 and approaching Tarbolton via the A 758.

Bachelors' Club

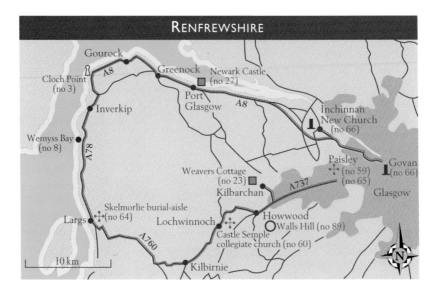

Skelmorlie Aisle: heraldic panel over the doorway

This excursion is designed for those staying in Glasgow and takes the visitor on a tour of Early Christian stones, and medieval and later sites in Renfrewshire.

Begin with the south-west of Scotland's most important collection of Early Christian sculpture which is housed in the Old Parish Church at Govan (no. 66). The church is not always open and it may be advisable to check with the minister in advance; alternatively ask at the Pearce Institute, a community centre, which stands in front of the church. Both the church (completed 1884) and the Pearce Institute (opened 1906) were designed by Sir R Rowand Anderson, who was also responsible for some of the restoration work at Dunblane Cathedral. The Pearce Institute was donated by the wife of the owner of Fairfields (now Kvaerner-Govan) Shipyard. For anyone wishing to see more of Govan, a Heritage Trail leaflet is available from Greater Glasgow Tourist Board.

Leave Govan on the A 8 and take a minor road to Inchinnan New Church (no. 68), where there are a further three Early Christian stones which complement those at Govan. Return to the A 8 and head for Port Glasgow, on the western outskirts of which stands Newark Castle (no. 27). Follow on around the coast through the striking 19th-century townscapes of Port Glasgow, Greenock and Gourock to the lighthouse ot Cloch Point (no. 3).

**Skelmorlie Aisle:
the Montgomery
Monument**

South of Cloch Point the A 78 hugs the Clyde coast past the power station at Inverkip down to Wemyss Bay Railway Station (no. 8) and on to the resort of Largs. In Largs, escape from the bustle of the town by seeking out the graveyard of the old parish church which contains the Skelmorlie burial aisle (no. 64).

The route now turns inland along the A 760 via Kilburnie to Lochwinnoch. Enter the town on the B 786 and approach Castle Semple Collegiate Church (no. 60) by a series of minor roads from Crossflat (NS 383609). Rejoin the A 737 at Howwood; then there is then a choice of sites: either climb up to the large iron-age fort at Walls Hill (no. 89) or visit the Weaver's Cottage (no. 23) at Kilbarchan with its working loom and teashop. If time permits, the excursion can end with a tour of Paisley Abbey (no. 59), which now also houses the Early Christian Cross from Barochan (no. 65).

Weaver's Cottage, Kilbarachan

Medieval drain serving Paisley Abbey

STIRLING

These two excursions are centred on the Forth valley and explore a wide range of medieval sites in and around Stirling, one of the principal seats of the Scottish Crown.

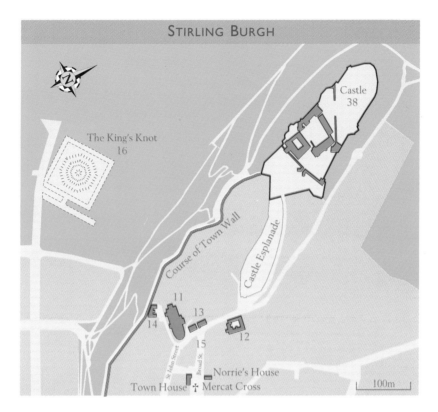

STIRLING BURGH

The King's Knot 16

Castle 38

Course of Town Wall

Castle Esplanade

11
13
14
15
12

St John Street
Broad St.

Norrie's House
Town House ✝ Mercat Cross

100m

The medieval burgh of Stirling retains many of its late medieval buildings clustered along the ridge in the lee of the castle. They form a compact group and can easily be visited on foot by the visitor staying in the town; for those coming by car, the Castle Esplanade car park provides a good starting point for the tour.

The castle (no. 38) is the focal point of the excursion. The panoramic views from the walls to the north, south, east and west demonstrate the strategic importance of the castle, and the pivotal role played by the castle in the middle ages is now well displayed for adults and children alike by the new exhibitions mounted by Historic Scotland. The visitor facilities at the castle have been greatly improved recently and include a cafe, as well as a shop.

After leaving the castle, walk down the ridge to view the buildings of the town. On the left is the grand house, known as the Argyll Lodging (no. 12); until recently this was a Youth Hostel and the interior is not currently open to the public but may soon be. Below the Argyll Lodging, but on the right hand side of the road, is Mar's Work, an unfinished house which, like Argyll's house, was designed for a courtier attached to the castle.

Stirling Castle

The Palace Block
(Below)

At Mar's Work the road divides and, on the left, Broad Street (no. 15) opens out to make use of the space available on the north side of the ridge for the market-place of the medieval burgh. Associated with the merchants houses that flank the street are the town house (town hall) and the mercat cross.

The town church, the Church of the Holy Rude (no. 11), stands at the head of Broad Street with, on its left, the former alms house, named Cowane's Hospital (no. 14) after its original benefactor. Instead of returning along the road, the esplanade can be reached by walking through the churchyard, passing on the right the 19th-century pyramidal monument to all those who suffered martyrdom in the cause of civil and religious liberty in Scotland.

For those with a car the tour can be extended by driving to the bottom of the town and visiting the Old Bridge (no. 17) over the Forth. From there it is a short drive to Cambuskenneth Abbey (no. 55), which was intimately connected with the royal events associated with the castle. Two other monuments associated with Stirling lie close by: the Wallace Monument (NS 819956) and the National Trust for Scotland's Bannockburn Centre (NS 797905).

Cambuskenneth Abbey: bell tower with Stirling Castle in the background (Top)

The bell tower

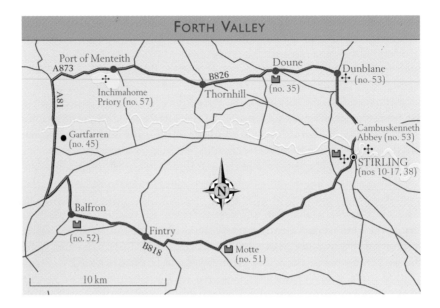

FORTH VALLEY

This excursion begins in Dunblane with a visit to the cathedral (no. 53) which also contains a Pictish cross-slab. Opposite the cathedral there is a small museum. The streets of the attractive town centre are narrow which makes parking difficult, but there is a carpark behind the cathedral.

From Dunblane take the A 820 to Doune, where the castle is well signposted to the left as the town is entered. Like Dunblane, Doune is a good example of a 19th-century Scottish townscape which has not suffered from over development nor has it been swamped by modern traffic.

Doune Castle

Turn southwards out of Doune on the A 84 and cross the narrow bridge over the River Teith before taking the second on the right (B 826) for Thornhill. Look out for the large cairn at Deanston (marked on the OS 1:50,000 map) after crossing the bridge. At Thornhill join the A 873, follow it along the northern flank of Flanders Moss until there is a Historic Scotland signpost for Inchmahome Priory (no. 57), then enjoy the short boat trip out to the island in the middle of the lake.

Visitors wishing to return directly to Stirling can do so by continuing southwards along the B 8034, which crosses the valley of the Forth and joins the main road (A 811) at Arnprior. For those with extra time, return to the Thorhhill road, turning left towards Aberfoyle to join the A 81 shortly before the town. At the junction turn left and, after crossing the Kelty Water look out for the homestead moat at Gartfarren (no. 45). Then take the A 811 and A 875 to Balfron and see the circular motte (no. 52) at the east end of the village. Finally, the day can be completed by looking at yet another type of medieval earthwork—the square motte of Sir John de Graham at Fintry (no. 51). To reach it follow the B 818, which continues to Denny and thence on to Stirling via the A 872.

Inchmahome Abbey:
from the air

SOUTH LANARKSHIRE

This contrasting pair of excursions looks at the monuments along the middle and upper reaches of the River Clyde, and, by using the motorway, they can be readily undertaken by visitors from Glasgow or by those staying further to the south.

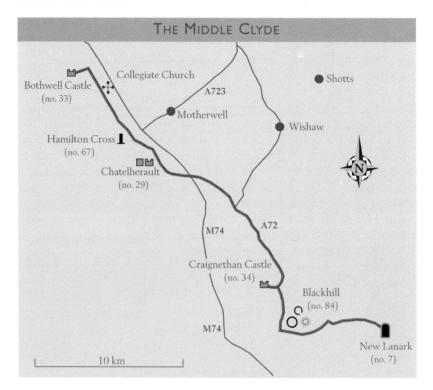

THE MIDDLE CLYDE

Bothwell Castle (no. 33)
Collegiate Church
A723
Shotts
Motherwell
Wishaw
Hamilton Cross (no. 67)
Chatelherault (no. 29)
N
A72
M74
Craignethan Castle (no. 34)
Blackhill (no. 84)
M74
New Lanark (no. 7)

10 km

Bothwell Castle:
from the air

Although the valley of the Clyde below Glasgow has been heavily industrialised in the last two centuries, it still contains a wealth of archaeological and historical monuments, and this excursion concentrates on the medieval and later sites, particularly those associated with the Hamilton family, but also includes the area's only World Heritage Site, the industrial village at New Lanark.

The excursion begins at Bothwell Castle (no. 33). Associated with the castle, and well worth a visit if open, is the Collegiate Church in Bothwell (NS 704585), which was founded by the third Earl of Douglas in 1397-98. Leave Bothwell for Hamilton on the B 7071 crossing Bothwell Bridge over the Clyde.

Once in Hamilton short detours can be made to look at the Early Christian cross (no. 67) and the Hamilton Mausoleum. The latter was begun in 1840 for the 10th Duke of Hamilton and was built to an original design by David Hamilton and completed by David Bryce. Hamilton Museum is situated by the turn off to the main road to the mausoleum.

Bothwell Castle

Leave Hamilton on the A 72 and follow the signposts for Chatelherault Country Park. The recently restored Garden House (no. 29) is the focal point of the park, but also included in the grounds are the ruins of the medieval stone castle of Cadzow and, further along the pleasant walk up the Avon Water, there is an early medieval earthwork castle, the precursor of the stone castle. Both these sites are identified on the park signboards.

From Chatelherault head for Craignethan Castle (no. 34) along the A 72 and follow the Historic Scotland signposts. After Craignethan the energetic might like to walk to the top of Black Hill, Lesmahagow (no. 84), otherwise rejoin the A 72 and make for Lanark and the signposts for New Lanark (no. 7). The mill village has been, and continues to be, restored; the buildings are of interest in their own right but the village also includes a number of displays and shops which make it a good venue for a rainy day.

Chatelherault

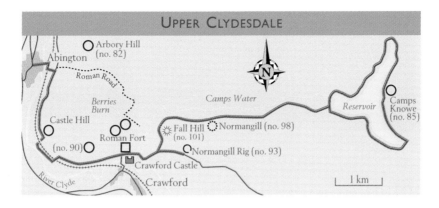

South of Lanark the industrial and urban landscapes of the middle Clyde give way to agricultural land fringed by uplands. Ploughing has destroyed many of the lower-lying sites but on the higher ground the sheep runs have percerved a remarkable cross-section of prehistoric ritual and settlement sites.

The excursion begins in Abington village (NS 931233). From there cross the River Clyde; the more energetic may wish to climb to the fort on Arbory Hill (no. 82), otherwise turn south and head for Crawford. Before reaching the settlement at Ritchie Ferry (no. 90) you will pass the fort at Castle Hill, set on an isolated knoll to the left of the road (NS 935218). After visiting the group of sites at Ritchie Ferry it is worth walking north-eastwards along the flanks of Castle and Raggengill Hills towards the fort at Berries Burn (NS 951218). About 100 m north-east of the fort there is a further site, this time a prehistoric homestead set within a bank which encloses the remains of at least one timber round house. The homestead lies on the bluff overlooking the Berries Burn, on the other side of which the Roman road from Carlisle rises out of the Clyde valley to climb around the back of Raggengill Hill whence it rejoins the valley south of Arbory. From Ritchie Ferry drive towards Castle Farm (NS 954213), and notice in passing the site of the Roman fort at Crawford which lies on the top of a slight rise north of the road and immediately west of the farm (NS 953214). On the opposite side of the road there are the remains of the motte and later tower of Crawford Castle. Continue along the road past Midlock and up the Camps Water as far as the henge at Normangill (no. 98). From there drive to the end of the public road, then take the private track round Camps Water Reservoir and climb the short distance up to the fort on Camps Knowe (no. 85). Follow on around the reservoir and retrace the route down the Camps Water as far as the road up the Midlock Water, turn left and head for the unenclosed platform settlement at Normangill Rig (no. 93); before returning to the car, walk on to the enclosed cremation cemetery (no. 101), which lies in the coll to the east of Fall Hill.

**Dumbarton
Castle**

Blackness Castle

Castle Campbell

**Glasgow
Cathedral, the
13th-century
choir**

Gardner's Warehouse, Glasgow (now Martin and Frost's); 1855-6, the first commercial building constructed using the prefabrication techniques pioneered at the Crystal Palace in London

Hutcheson's Hall, Glasgow, built in 1802 by the young David Hamilton, who was to become one of Glasgow's greatest architects

TRANSPORT AND INDUSTRY

Postcard from the Tenement House: sailing 'doon the watter'

The area covered by this volume includes the Glasgow conurbation which encompasses the industrial heartland of Scotland. Consequently the landscapes and townscapes are full of monuments to the industrial heritage, and described in this section are a selection of monuments accessible, or open, to the public, which illustrate the range of industries and their supporting infrastructure over the last two centuries.

In recent decades Scotland has lost much of its industrial heritage but, after years of neglect, interest in industrial archaeology is steadily growing. This is due both to the work of industrial archaeologists and as a by-product of the renewed appreciation of the fine Victorian architecture of many of the factories and mills. Thus, while it is necessary to preserve monuments such as the Biggar Gas Works (no. 2) as site museums, it was possible to save New Lanark (no. 7) and Templeton's Carpet Factory (no. 9) by sympathetically converting them into modern industrial units.

Alloa Glass Works: the destroyed glass cone

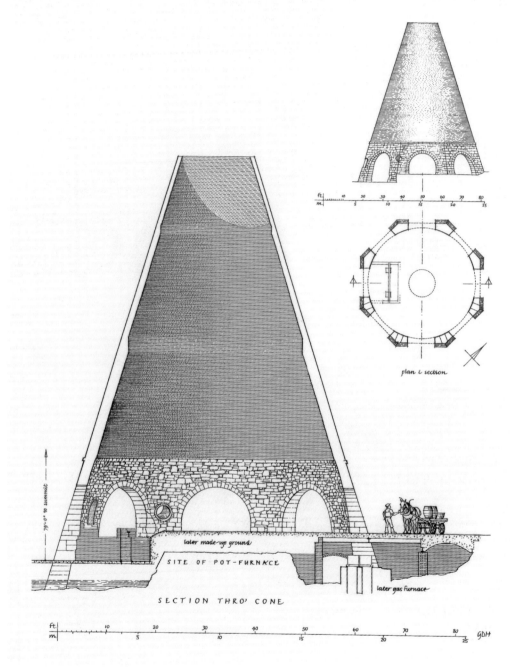

Alloa Glass Works: drawing of the glass cone

1* Alloa Glass Cone, Clackmannan

19th century.

NS 881923. The glass works lie in the S of the town off Glassworks Loan. The factory is still in use and permission to visit should be sought at the gate.

Glass making was introduced to Alloa in 1750 by Lady Francis Erskine who persuaded a number of glassworkers to come from Bohemia to establish a works in the town. The factory has remained in production ever since and, although most of the plant is modern, it still retains a 19th-century brick glass cone which is the last surviving example of its type in Scotland.

Biggar Gas Works: the retorts

2* Biggar Gas Works, South Lanarkshire

Mid to late 19th century.

NT 038375. The gas works lies NW of the town centre and is signposted from the High Street (A702).

National Museums of Scotland/Historic Scotland.

Biggar Gas Works is one of the last surviving examples of a small town gas works which were once familiar sights throughout Scotland, and it has recently been taken over by the Royal Museum of Scotland. It comprises a group of single-storey buildings accompanied by two gas-holders, the larger with five guides and the smaller with three. The retorts are of horizontal type and are housed in a building with a Belfast roof.

3* The Cloch Lighthouse, Inverkip, Inverclyde

AD 1797.

NS 203758. The Cloch Lighthouse lies immediately W of the Gourock to Inverkip road (A 78) about 4.5 km SW of Gourock.

Not open to the public.

The Cloch is one of the three lighthouses built to protect the difficult waters at the head of the Firth of Clyde, the other two being on Little Cumbrae and at Toward Point, Cowal. Increased traffic on the Clyde in the later 18th century led to demands from Glasgow shipowners for more lights on the river; consequently, in 1795 Cloch Point was chosen as 'unquestionably the most proper situation' and the light was first shown on 11th August 1797. A Greenock river pilot, Allan McLean, was selected as the first keeper at a salary of £30 p.a. and, besides his duties as a keeper, he was allowed to continue to act as a pilot, so long as this did not interfere with his other duties.

The lighthouse was built by Kermack and Gall; it consists of a short, round tower with corbelled walkways, and it is now accompanied by two sets of keepers' houses. The earlier houses are used as stores and the later are easily identified by their crowstepped gables.

Cloch Lighthouse: c.1920

Devon Colliery:

the engine house

detail of the beam

(Below)

4* Devon Colliery Engine House, Fishcross, Clackmannan

AD 1865.

NS 898958. Devon Colliery lies to the NW of Fishcross on a minor road that links the B 9140 with the A 91.

Although the Devon Colliery is now closed, the Beam Engine House has been preserved and partially restored as a monument to the industrial history of Clackmannan. Erected in 1865, this ashlar-built engine house contains one of the few remaining beam engines in Scotland. It was made by Neilson and Co, Glasgow and was used to pump water from the coal-workings.

5 Forth and Clyde Canal

Late 18th century.

NS 927826 to 449735. The canal is readily accessible for much of its course, and visitors will find the OS 2½ inch map of the Antonine Wall a useful guide as the two monuments run side by side by for long stretches.

The Forth and Clyde Canal is one of Scotland's three ship, rather than barge, canals (the other two being the Caledonian and the Crinan) and, according to the preamble to its Parliamentary Act, it was designed to 'open an easy communication between the Firths of Forth and Clyde, as also between the interior parts of the country, which will not only be a great advantage to the trade carried on between the said two Firths, but will

Forth and Clyde Canal: drawing of canal office, Port Dundas (Right)

also tend to the improvements of the adjacent lands, the relief of the poor, and the preservation of the public roads, and moreover be of general utility'. Construction began at the east end in 1768, with the first section opening in 1773. Work was then interrupted by financial difficulties, and Robert Whitworth replaced John Smeaton as engineer for the construction of the western section (1787-90), which ran from Kirkintilloch to Bowling. The canal remained in use until 1962, when it was finally closed to freight traffic.

The canal was built from Grangemouth on the Forth to Bowling on the Clyde, and it had a branch line running into the basin in the centre of Glasgow at Port Dundas (NS 588666). At water level the canal was 19.2 m in mean breadth by 2.9 m in depth, and the locks were 21 m long by 6 m broad. Since closure, many of the canal installations have been altered or demolished but features of interest may still be seen at: Falkirk/Camelon: locks 9-11 and 12-16, NS 868800 to 881806. Falkirk: Union Inn at the junction of the Forth and Clyde and Union Canals, NS 868800. Wyndford: lock 20, NS 776787. Kirkintilloch: aqueduct over the Luggie Water, NS 657739. Glasgow: Kelvin Aqueduct (1787-90), NS 561689. Maryhill: locks, NS 563690. Knightswood: locks, NS 534705. Port Dundas: canal office, NS 588666. Dalmuir West: bascule bridge (hinged at one side to allow ships to pass under it), NS 478713. Ferrydyke: bascule bridge, NS 458730. Bowling: sealocks, basin, bascule bridge, railway swing- bridge, and custom house, NS 450735.

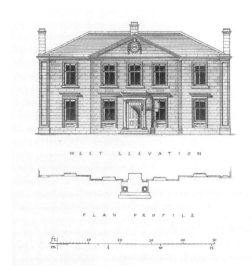

WEST ELEVATION

PLAN PROFILE

6 Muirkirk, MacAdam's Tar Workings, East Ayrshire

Late 18th and early 19th century.

NS 6925. From Muirkirk (A 70) take the side road south, signposted to Kames, and follow the track which the road eventually becomes, as far as the cairn marked on the 1:50,000 map.

From the late 18th until the middle of the 20th century Muirkirk lay at the heart of the Scottish iron industry. A plentiful source of coal, from relatively shallow workings, combined with high grade iron ore, and readily available limestone for flux, as well as a copious supply of water, meant that Muirkirk was ideally suited for the production of iron, and the industrial archaeological landscape which extends for many hundreds of metres on the south side of the A 70 bears witness to the exploitation of these natural resources for almost two centuries.

Although there was coal and iron working in Muirkirk at an earlier date, the industry expanded rapidly in the last quarter of the 18th century following the establishment, in 1786, of a tar works by Archibald Cochrane; the lease was later bought by John Loudon MacAdam, who is perhaps best remembered for his work as a road engineer. One of the principal by-products of tar production was coke; this was an ideal fuel for iron smelting and, in 1787, a group of iron masters founded an iron works to exploit this added bonus.

The area shown on the map and in the photograph represents only a small part of this vast site but encapsulates most of the principal features, with the addition of the footings of the tarworks which by good fortune have survived since going out of use in 1809. Their most obvious feature is a bank of distillation kilns which have been set into a natural terrace to the rear of the still-house and other buildings to the east of the track. To the south of the tarworks there is an area of early coal working, with the shafts surrounded by a ring of spoil and, in some cases, the traces of a horse-gang for hauling up the coal visible on the top of the spoil. Also visible are fragments of tramways which linked the various shafts and carried the coal away to the iron and tarworks. To the west of the trackway, north-west of the tarworks, there are the footings of a miners row. These provided basic accommodation for the miners and were sometimes accompanied by small gardens for growing vegetables.

Many of the shafts are uncapped and the visitor should take care when walking around this fascinating site.

Forth and Clyde Canal: Maryhill, Glasgow, aquaduct from the west (Left)

MacAdam's Tarworks, Muirkirk: aerial view

MacAdam's Tarworks, Muirkirk

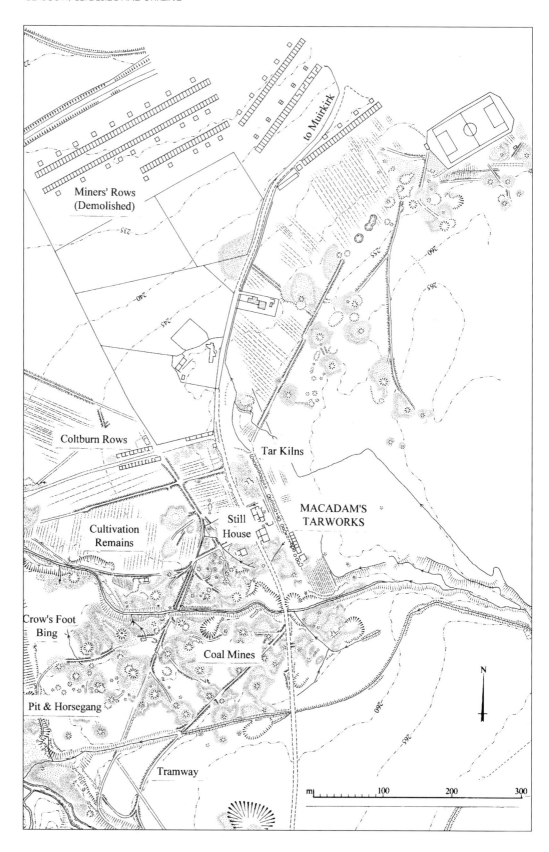

Miners' Rows (Demolished)

to Muirkirk

Coltburn Rows

Tar Kilns

Cultivation Remains

Still House

MACADAM'S TARWORKS

Crow's Foot Bing

Coal Mines

Pit & Horsegang

Tramway

N

m| 100   200   300

7 New Lanark Industrial Village, South Lanarkshire

Late 18th and early 19th century.

NS 880426. The village of New Lanark lies on the N bank of the River Clyde 1 km S of Lanark and is well signposted from Lanark town centre.

The village of New Lanark has justifiably been described as 'the outstanding industrial monument in Scotland', for it not only contains an unrivalled collection of late 18th century and early 19th century mills, workers' houses and public buildings, but was also the scene of Robert Owen's famous attempt to humanise the industrial revolution. The mills remained in use until 1968, after which they rapidly became derelict but were saved from demolition by the New Lanark Conservation and Civic Trust. The Trust co-ordinated the efforts of several interested groups and the majority of the work of restoration has been carried out by local unemployed youngsters. One of the first projects they tackled was the renovation of the Nursery Buildings, which subsequently won a Scottish Civic Trust award. Over the last ten years the village has been slowly brought back to life and now has a growing residential population supported by a number of small industries.

The original mills were established on the banks of the Clyde in 1784 to harness the power of the river and were founded by David Dale (a Glasgow banker) and his partner Richard Arkwright (the pioneer of mechanical spinning). By 1798, when

Robert Owen was appointed manager, the village was already a thriving concern forming the largest collection of cotton mills in Scotland. During the next twenty years Owen expanded the work of the mills and introduced a series of radical social reforms, which greatly improved working conditions and turned New Lanark into a showplace drawing 20,000 visitors between 1815 and 1825.

Owen's concern for the well being, and therefore efficiency, of the workforce is reflected in the buildings erected during his period of management. In 1809 the Nursery was built to house 300 pauper apprentices who until then had been expected to sleep in the mill beside their machines. Four years later, in 1813, the Store was opened to improve the standard of goods available to the workers; it was run on co-operative lines and ensured that profiteering did not occur. One of Owen's principal interests was education, and two buildings

commemorate this. The Institute for the Formation of Character (1816) served as library, reading room, canteen, dancehall and place of worship; it was open to all the staff and their families, filling the function of a modern community centre. Equally important was the School, founded in 1817, which was Scotland's first school for infants. Other buildings of note are the Counting House and the New Buildings.

8 Wemyss Bay Station and Pier, North Ayrshire

AD 1903.

NS 193685. Wemyss Bay Station lies on the W side of the A 78 between the village of Wemyss Bay and Skelmorlie.

Wemyss Bay station and its pier were renowned to generations of Glaswegians as the railway terminus for their annual trip 'doon the watter' to Rothesay on the island of Bute.

Originally opened in 1865 by the Wemyss Bay Railway Company, the station was completely rebuilt in 1903 by its new owners, the Caledonian Railway Company, and is regarded as one of the finest stations of its period. From the outside it is distinguished by its clock-tower and from the inside by the centrally placed booking office from which radiate the steel ribs for the glazed roof.

Wemyss Bay Station

The booking hall
(Right)

TOWNS AND TOWNSCAPE

Glasgow: central
gridscape

Only two towns, Glasgow and Stirling, have been given detailed treatment
in this volume and they have been chosen to represent two key elements in
the development of Scottish towns and townscape, ie the foundation of the
medieval burghs and 19th-century industrial expansion.

A high proportion of the present number of towns in Scotland were given
the taxation and trading advantages of burgh status during the middle ages
(beginning in the 12th century), either by the Crown or by the local feudal
superior, as a deliberate attempt to foster trade and therefore taxable
revenue. Many of these towns rested on earlier foundations (cf Stirling) and
most have continued to be occupied to the present day. Their fortunes,
however, varied greatly; some like Lanark, Falkirk, Hamilton, Paisley, Ayr
and Stirling have continued to expand and flourish, while others have
remained small (Airth, Kincardine, Clackmannan, Biggar, Carnwath,
Mauchline and Maybole, to name but a few). Most of the latter retain
much of their medieval street plan and contain interesting examples of
17th- and 18th-century domestic buildings.

From the last quarter of the 18th century a number of towns, particularly those in the central belt, began to grow rapidly as trade in textiles and the iron and steel industries expanded. Glasgow swallowed up many of the surrounding burghs to become Scotland's first conurbation. The rush of population to the towns had begun, and in its wake produced some of the worst housing conditions in Europe with the poorer Glasgow tenements a by-word for slums. At the same time, and in stark contrast, much time and money was spent on public works which have left many of the industrial towns with magnificent Victorian municipal buildings and churches, the true value of which is only now being appreciated and restored (particularly in Glasgow).

Trade and industry were not, however, the only reasons for the foundation or growth of towns, The presence of the Glasgow conurbation led to the development of tourism along the Clyde coast and the rapid expansion of small burghs and villages from Inverkip in Renfrew to Ballantrae in the south of Ayrshire. These towns have a bright and breezy air and contain some interesting examples of late Victorian and Edwardian townscape. Their growth was linked with the spread of the railway system and cruising on the Clyde steamers, and this relationship is exemplified in the railway station and pier at Wemyss Bay (no. 8).

Overcrowding in Glasgow and the development of an efficient railway system encouraged the better-off Victorian and Edwardian professional classes to live outside the city, and a number of commuter towns grew up, particularly to the west. Kilmacolm, Renfrew, is typical of these towns with its large number of detached villas, some of which were designed by distinguished architects such as Charles Rennie Mackintosh.

The deliberate fostering of towns did not cease with the medieval burghs but continued in various guises into the present century. The rigid grid-pattern of central Helensburgh and Ardrossan are examples of 18th-century town planning, while the more open plan of the attractive village of Eaglesham, Renfrew, also laid out in the 18th-century, shows a contrasting style more appropriate to its rural setting. Strathclyde can also boast of three of Scotland's 20th-century new towns, and Cumbernauld, East Kilbride and Irvine are witness to the importance of the motor car in modern urban design.

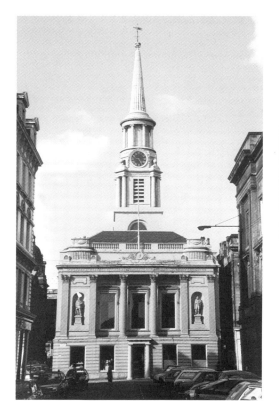

9 Glasgow

Although Glasgow achieved burgh status as early as the 12th century, the present city owes little to the medieval period (but see the Cathedral, no. 54, and the nearby Provan Lordship), and it is largely a creation of the last two centuries. The boom decades of the Victorian era have bequeathed to Glasgow one of Europe's most extensive 19th-century townscapes and a unique range of Victorian architecture. Glasgow may not have been the political capital of Scotland but it was the commercial centre, and vast sums were spent on prestigious building projects, particularly by industrial concerns, banks and the city itself. On the darker side, the wretchedness of much of the mass housing must not be overlooked (but see the Tenement, no. 22) and driving around Glasgow the visitor cannot fail to miss the rapid and stark contrast between various parts of the city.

The medieval town lay to the north of the Clyde, well above the river, and was centred around the crossing of two principal thoroughfares—the west-east Argyle Street/Trongate/Gallowgate and the north-south High Street/Saltmarket Street. Rapid growth at the end of the 18th and beginning of the 19th centuries led to expansion to the north-west of the medieval town and to development on the south side of the river. These areas were laid out on a rigid rectangular grid pattern (in what we might today consider to be typically American style), which still forms a characteristic feature of the city centre. In later 19th-century developments, such as those around Park Circus, Kelvinside, the rigidity of the grid pattern was softened by the use of crescents and circuses.

The public architecture of the city centre is a mixture of styles, ranging from severe classical to flamboyant Baroque and Gothic, which manage to knit together to form a comparatively harmonious townscape. Running through all the various historical moods, however, Glasgow manages to achieve a recognisable local style: of particular note are the works of Alexander (Greek) Thomson (St Vincent Street Church), Charles Rennie Mackintosh (Glasgow School of Art, Scotland Street School, Willow Tea Rooms) and the cast-iron buildings (Gardner's Warehouse, Ca D'Oro). Listed below is a selection of the principal buildings in the city.

Townscape

The City Centre: George Square, Buchanan Street, St Vincent Street, Blythswood Square.
Later Victorian Town Planning: Park Circus/Woodlands (NS 575663).
Restoration in the Woodlands area won an Urban Renaissance Award.
Great Western Road (NS 5667).

Glasgow: University of Glasgow, c.1900

Glasgow: Hutcheson Hall (Left)

Glasgow: City Chambers, George Square, c.1900

Glasgow: St Vincent Street Church

Public Architecture

City Chambers, George Square. 1833, recently cleaned, with magnificent interiors.
Clydesdale Bank, St Vincent Street. 1870, recently restored, built in ornamental Baroque style.
Hutchesons Hall; Ingram Street. 1802-5. Glasgow Headquarters of the National Trust for Scotland.
Stock Exchange, Buchanan Street. 1877, secular Gothic style.
St Vincent Street Church. 1859, Alexander (Greek) Thomson's strange mixture of Greek temple with Egyptian details.

Glasgow: School of Art, Renfrew Street (Right)

Charles Rennie Mackintosh

Glasgow School of Art, Renfrew Street. 1897-1907, Mackintosh's finest building.
Scotland Street School.
Willow Tea Rooms, Sauchiehall Street. 1903, recently restored and now used as a jewelry shop.
5 Blythswood Square, Art Nouveau doorway.
Hunterian Art Gallery, Hillhead Street. Mackintosh interiors.

Education and Leisure

The University, Hillhead. 1874, Gilbert Scott with Gothic Revival.
Glasgow Art Gallery and Museum, Kelvingrove. 1901, a legacy of the Glasgow International Exhibition.
Botanical Gardens, Kelvinside. 1873. Magnificent glasshouse, known as Kibble Palace, after the architect John Kibble.
Burrell Museum, Pollock Park. 1982, much praised modern museum.

Cast-Iron Buildings

Ca D'Oro, Buchanan Street. 1872.
Gardner's Warehouse, Jamaica Street. 1862, designed by John Gardner, also known as 'The Iron Building'.

Factory

Templeton's Carpet Factory, Glasgow Green. 1889, loosely derived from the Doge's Palace in Venice, the colourful design helps to brighten up this part of Glasgow. Now converted to small commercial units.

10 Stirling

Stirling was one of the principal burghs of medieval Scotland, and the core of the burgh survives as one of the county's best remaining examples of a medieval street plan. In addition, it contains a major collection of 16th and 17th-century buildings that reflect its importance as a royal centre in the late medieval period.

Like its rival Edinburgh, Stirling is dominated by a royal castle (no. 38), and the town developed on a restricted site along the crest of a glacially sculpted ridge in the lee of the castle. The town occupies a nodal position at the highest tidal reach of the Forth (like Perth on the Tay) which also coincides with the lowest bridging point of the river (for a description of the medieval bridge, see no. 17), making it the furthest navigable port for sea-going craft. The significance of sea-borne transport and trade should not be overlooked in the medieval period, and Stirling's position can be contrasted with that of the late medieval royal centre at Linlithgow, West Lothian, where it was necessary to protect its port, Blackness, with a castle (no. 32). Thus Stirling stood at the junction of major land and sea routes, but the success of the burgh also depended on the presence of the royal castle. The town flourished as the royal court continued to be held there, and it enjoyed a golden age from the 15th to the 17th centuries, but with the union of the crowns Stirling's importance waned. When prosperity picked up again in the 19th century, the focus of settlement shifted away from the Castle Rock to lower ground and in doing so saved the medieval core from major redevelopment.

Stirling: St Ninian's, Old Parish Church, west tower

The Castle Rock has probably been occupied continuously since prehistoric times, but no trace of pre-Norman civil settlement has been found and the only evidence for use during the early historic period comes from documentary references. Stirling was one of the earliest towns to achieve burgh status, and it was probably granted this privilege by David I during the first half of the 13th century. The main axis of the medieval town lay along the crest of the ridge (the modern Castle Wynd, St John Street, Spittal Street, Baker Street, King Street) with the Church of the Holy Rude (no. 11) standing on high ground above the principal street (Broad Street). Although the street pattern was probably established during the High Middle Ages, no buildings of this period survive, and excavation in other Scottish medieval burghs has suggested that most buildings would have been of timber. Stone replaced timber as the main building material during the 16th and 17th centuries, and it is to this period that most of the important buildings in the medieval town belong. A particular feature of Stirling are the town houses of the 16th and 17th centuries, ranging from those of courtiers (Argyll Lodging no. 12 and Mar's Work no. 13) to lesser houses belonging to town burgesses (Norrie's House, Broad Street, no. 15, and Cowane's House in St Mary's Wynd). The most important buildings and monuments in the town are described in detail below.

In the 18th and 19th centuries development took place on the lower ground away from the historic core of the burgh. As the town expanded, it incorporated outlying villages including St Ninians with its fine church steeple built in 1734. The Victorian town centre has been much altered, but there are attractive late 19th-century residential areas still surviving on the west side of the town.

11 Church of the Holy Rude, Stirling

15th to 20th centuries.

NS 792937. The church lies on the W side of the junction of Castle Wynd and St John's Street, immediately S of Mar's Work.

The Church of the Holy Rude was the parish church of the medieval burgh, and its large size and imposing design reflect the importance of the town

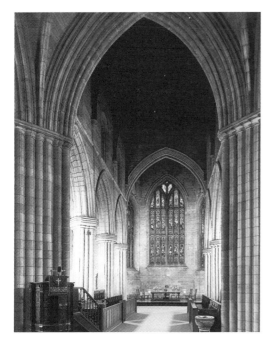

in late medieval times. Records show that there was a church in the burgh from at least as early as the 12th century, but the present building was not begun until 1456.

Work on the church was divided into two phases, presumably to help to defray the considerable costs of erecting such a large building. The nave was built first and was completed sometime in the 1470s; it is rectangular on plan, with north and south flanking aisles of five bays each, and it has a centrally placed tower at the west end. To this simple design wealthy burgesses soon added chantry chapels, which comprised rectangular projections from the aisle bays. Of the three originally built, only St Andrew's Aisle (dating from before 1483) now survives, the other two having been removed in the course of later building work.

The second stage of the work began soon after 1507, with the construction of the chancel. It was to consist of projecting transepts with a substantial tower placed above the crossing, a choir which continued the form of the nave, and an apsidal presbytery attached to the east of the choir. Construction was slow, and work appears to have stopped by 1546 before the transepts or tower had been completed. In the 17th century a dispute among the parishioners led to the church being partitioned and the formation of two separate congregations. Further extensive internal and external changes were carried out early in the 19th century, greatly altering the character of the medieval work. At the beginning of the present century it was decided to undo some of the damage wrought during the past 150 years: between 1911-14 and 1936-40 the internal arrangements of the building were restored, as far as possible, to those of the late medieval church, and the transepts, originally planned in 1507, were finally added.

There are no medieval burial monuments visible in the graveyard, but it contains a large number of 18th and 19th-century gravestones and memorials whose inscriptions testify to the activity of the townsfolk and surrounding landowners and farmers. The most surprising of these monuments is in the form of a pyramid situated close to the wall of the Castle Esplanade.

Holy Rude Church, Stirling: the choir from the crossing (Top Left)

From the south-east (Top)

12 Argyll's Lodging, Stirling

16th to 17th centuries.

NS 792932. This house fronts on to the side of Castle Wynd about half way along its course.

Historic Scotland.

Argyll's Lodging has been described as 'the most important surviving town house of its period in

Argyll's Lodging, Stirling, the courtyard

doorway to the staircase-tower in the south-west angle of the courtyard. A century later the house was sold by the 4th Duke of Argyll and ultimately passed to the Crown who are still responsible for its guardianship.

13 Mar's Work, Stirling

Late 16th century.

NS 792937. Mar's Work lies at the south end of Castle Wynd on the west side of the street facing the top of Broad Street.

Historic Scotland.

The sad remains of this once large and important Renaissance mansion have been reduced to a single, roughly rectangular block, fronting on to Castle Wynd. Originally there were wings on the north and south which enclosed three sides of a rectangular courtyard, but the foundations of these are now buried under the graveyard of the Church of the Holy Rude (no. 11). Unlike its near neighbour, Argyll's Lodging (no. 12), Mar's Work is essentially a one-period building, erected for the Earl of Mar between 1570 and 1572. Mar became Regent of Scotland in 1571, but died in the following year before the house was finished, and it appears that it was never, in fact, completed. In 1733 the Town Council took a lease on the site in order to turn it into a workhouse (cf the plans to turn Argyll's Lodging into an almshouse); by 1777, however, the house was roofless and in a ruinous condition.

Scotland' and earns this reputation on account of its good state of preservation and the architectural quality of the building. Originally built in the 16th century, it was acquired by the Crown about 1800, serving as a military hospital until the 1950s and has until recently been used as a Youth Hostel.

Although the house gives the superficial impression of belonging to a single phase, it underwent a long period of building and alteration beginning in the 16th century, and reaching its apogee in 1674. Today, the building is ranged around three sides of an irregular courtyard, while the fourth side, which includes the entrance gateway, is enclosed by a screen-wall. The earliest part of the building forms the ground-floor of the north-east side of the court; this was later expanded to the south to form an L-shaped block, and subsequently the main north range was extended. About 1630 the site was acquired by William Alexander, Viscount Stirling, a prominent courtier of Charles I, who carried out extensive alterations including the construction of the east range and the modification of the south block. Alexander died in 1640 and, following his death, the house was taken over by the Town Council with a view to converting it to an almshouse (see also Mar's Work, no. 13), but in 1666 the site was bought by Archibald, 9th Earl of Argyll. The Earl finished the south range in 1674, and the completion of the project is commemorated in a datestone which lies over the

Mar's Work, Stirling (Right)

The principal feature of the building is the lavish decoration of the facade. In contrast with the rich

Anglo-Netherlandish style of Argyll's Lodging, Mar's Work reflects the less flamboyant Renaissance style of design that had been introduced to Scotland from France in the 1530s. Mar was doubtless following the fashion set by James V's Palace Block in Stirling Castle (no. 38).

Apart from the twin towers that flank the entrance pend, the facade is flat, but it was richly ornamented with carving that is now much weathered. The decoration includes: heraldic and inscribed panels, initial letters and dummy gargoyles in the form of cannon. High above the door archway there is a large heraldic panel which, amongst other devices, bears the royal arms of Scotland, indicating that Mar was a Crown vassal, thus entitling him to place the royal arms, in this case those of James (Jacobus) VI, above his own.

---

14 Cowane's Hospital, Stirling

Mid 17th century.

NS 791936. Cowane's Hospital lies at the west end of the short street that flanks the south side of the Church of the Holy Rude.

John Cowane was a wealthy merchant who, on his death in 1633, left a sum of 40.000 merks for the construction of an almshouse or hospital to house 'tuelf (twelve) decayed guidbroder, burgessis and

induellors' of the burgh of Stirling. The building is still in public use, although no longer as an almshouse, and consequently it is not possible to view the interior.

The hospital is E-shaped on plan with a projecting bell-tower at the centre of the principal facade, an unusual form for Scotland at this period. Work was begun in May 1637 but not finally completed until 1648 when the statue of John Cowane was placed over the entrance. We know rather more about the construction of this building than most others of the period, as the building accounts still survive. It was designed by no less a person than the Master Mason to the Crown, John Mylne, and the work was carried out under the supervision of James Rynd, a Stirling mason. Some of the stone was newly quarried and brought from Plean and Dunmore, a little to the east of the town, while other loads were robbed from the ruins of Cambuskenneth Abbey (see no. 55) on the opposite shore of the Forth.

Most of the original internal fittings were removed in 1852 when the building was converted for use as a guildhall, but parts of the garden remain with a small flagged terrace on the east leading to a bowling-green. The Hospital is not Stirling's only reminder of John Cowane, as his house still survives in the town and its facade can be seen at the bottom of St Mary's Wynd.

Cowane's Hospital, Stirling

15 Broad Street, Stirling

17th and 18th centuries.

NS 792937.

Broad Street (formerly called Market Street) was the principal street of the medieval town and, despite its somewhat restrained air today, still retains much of the character of a late medieval market street with its merchants' houses, tolbooth and mercat cross.

Unlike the courtyard houses of the nobility in Castle Wynd (Mar's Work and Argyll's Lodging, nos 12 and 13), the houses of the merchants and burgesses are tightly crammed together with only the gable end projecting on to the street front. The earlier medieval houses would have been of timber and these were replaced in stone during the course of 16th and 17th centuries. Much alteration has

**Town House,
Broad Street,
Stirling**

taken place since then, but the street-line and the plots have been fossilised. The narrow street facades offered the only opportunity for a public display of individual architectural detail, and the proud owners of these houses frequently advertised their status and wealth by embellishing their frontages. Much of this detail has been lost over the centuries but the best surviving example lies at No. 34, which is known after its 17th-century owner as Norrie's House. James Norrie was Town Clerk and, from a date-stone on the building, he appears to have had the house built in 1671. It is four storeys high with an attic and is built of large ashlar blocks. The single gabled facade finishes in crowsteps and is crowned by a finial carved in the form of a human head. There are three windows on each floor (the original doorway is missing and it is now entered from next door), and above each there is a triangular pediment containing texts and initials, which include (on the first floor) ARBOR VITAE SAPIENTIA (Wisdom is the tree of life) and MURUS AHENEUS: BONA CONSCIENTIA (A good conscience is a brazen wall), and on the second floor SOL(LI) DEO GLORIA (Glory to God alone) which is flanked by the initials (IN and AR) of James Norrie and his wife Agnes Robertson.

Opposite Norrie's House stands the Town House or Tolbooth, the administrative centre of the town. Originally built in 1703-5 to a design of the distinguished Scots architect Sir William Bruce, it was extended in 1785 and again between 1806-11, when a jail and courthouse were added. It has the distinction of being one of the earliest tolbooths to have been built in the classical style and the dubious honour of being copied by the Alloa mason, Tobias Bauchop, when he built the Mid-Steeple in Dumfries.

A further reminder of the commercial connections of Broad Street is the Mercat Cross which stands in the middle of the carriageway in front of the Town House. It was re-erected here in 1891 following its removal by the Town Council in 1792. Only the unicorn finial, affectionately known locally as 'Puggy', is original, the shaft having been added as part of the Victorian restoration. The unicorn is sitting, and in front of its breast there is a crowned shield bearing the royal arms of Scotland, as befitting a royal burgh, and it is surrounded by the collar of the Order of the Thistle, the premier order of chivalry in Scotland.

16 The King's Knot, Stirling

Early 17th century.

NS 789934. The King's Knot can be entered either from the Dumbarton Road (A 811), or from the Castle Esplanade by following the signposted footpath down the face of Castle Rock.

Historic Scotland.

The King's Knot forms the most prominent part of an elaborate landscaped garden laid out in 1628-9 as a part of a programme of alterations carried out at Stirling Castle for Charles I. It is situated at the foot of Castle Rock and lies in the north-east corner of The King's Park which, since the end of the 12th century, had been enclosed as a royal hunting park.

The gardens consisted of an orchard, a large rectangular parterre (an area of garden laid out with formal flower beds) and, attached to the south-east side of the latter, a double-ditched enclosure containing an octagonal mound known as The Knot. Formal gardens of this type were fashionable in the 17th century and their layouts were influenced by English Elizabethan and Jacobean designs. The parterre and knot enclosures are both rectangular and both are divided into four major quadrants with central features. In the case of the parterre, the rectangle is again subdivided into four quadrants with a circular central bed. Thus the design of the two sections of the formal garden complement one another and, doubtless, their relationship would have been enhanced by the lay-out of their respective flower-beds. Of the latter no trace survives, but we can be fairly certain that the plantings would have consisted of geometric designs, possibly combined with beds in the form of monograms or lettering, and that much use would have been made of topiary and low box hedges to edge borders or to form patterns on their own. An idea of how such a garden would have appeared can be gained by visiting the replanted garden at Pitmedden Castle, Aberdeenshire (NTS) and, on a smaller scale, the replanted garden at Chatelherault (no. 29).

King's Knot, Stirling

Despite all the effort to construct the gardens, they were not maintained for long and by the beginning of the 18th century they had fallen into disuse, in part due to the Crown's failure to use Stirling Castle as a major residence. A 'thorough restoration and renewal' was accomplished in 1867; unfortunately this involved much alteration to the gardens, including remodelling The Knot and possibly realigning The Knot enclosure.

17 Old Bridge, Stirling

Late 15th/early 16th century.

NS 797945. The bridge can be approached from either side of the Forth; from the S along the Drip Road (A84) or from the N along the Perth Road (A9).

Historic Scotland.

The Old Bridge at Stirling is the best preserved of the two surviving late medieval bridges in the former county of Stirling (the other being at Bannockburn, NS 807904). Until comparatively recent times, Stirling was the lowest bridging point on the Forth, and the town owed much of its importance in medieval times to the strategic value

of this position. Like the houses of the earlier medieval town, the first bridges across the Forth were of wood (despite the misleading representation of a stone bridge on the burgh seal of 1296), and in 1905 the foundations of a wooden bridge were found in the river bed about 60 m upstream of the Old Bridge.

The present bridge, probably the first to be built of stone, dates from the late 15th century or early 16th century. It spans the river with four semicircular arches supported on piers with triangular cut-waters. On the sides of the carriageway there are refuges for pedestrians which, until the 18th century, were roofed. Originally the ends of the bridge were provided with archways, and the one on the north side of the river had an iron gate, but they were removed in the 18th century and replaced by small square pillars.

In 1745 one of the arches was cut on the orders of General Blakeney in order to prevent the Jacobite army from entering the town, but the damage was soon repaired and the bridge continued in use until 1831, when a new bridge was built about 100 m downstream.

Old Bridge, Stirling

HOUSES GREAT AND SMALL

Souter Johnnie's Cottage, Kirkoswald: the workshop

No examples of the types of buildings that would have housed the mass of the rural or urban population during the medieval period have survived intact. Their remains, however, can occasionally be seen in the countryside or are unearthed in the course of urban excavations. Wood, wattle, clay and turf were the major building materials, and these continued in use into the 18th century when they were superseded by stone, and it is only from this date that substantial numbers of houses, either in the countryside or towns, survive.

For most of the medieval period the upper echelons of society found it necessary to occupy defended sites, and these castles and tower-houses are dealt with elsewhere. From the 16th century onwards, however, more peaceful conditions made it possible for the nobility and gentry to abandon the restricted defensive sites in favour of more spacious types of accommodation. This was a gradual process and it took some two centuries before the medieval tradition was supplanted. In many cases, particularly in the 16th and 17th centuries, additional accommodation was provided by building a new wing on to an existing tower. This process can be seen at Castle Campbell (no. 39) and at Newark (no. 27), while at Kinneil (no. 26) the Palace was built to replace the destroyed medieval tower. The two former sites still retained a defensive courtyard wall, as did the hunting lodge at Provan Hall (no. 28), and the laird's house at Craignethan Castle (no. 34) made use of the outer court wall of the abandoned castle. It was not until the late 17th and early 18th centuries that defence ceased to play a significant role in house design, opening the way for the great age of country houses in the late 18th and 19th centuries. Culzean (no. 25) and Brodick (no. 24) typify the two key elements in the development of country houses: the former representing the old established agricultural estate and the latter the sporting estates which played such an important part in the Highlands in the 19th century.

Many of the great houses were accompanied by fine gardens and policies (parkland), most of which date from the 18th and 19th centuries (Culzean, Brodick and Chatelherault), but earlier examples can also be found at Stirling (The King's Knot, no. 16), Castle Campbell (no. 39) and Inchmahome Priory (no. 57). The gardens were practical as well as decorative, and walled gardens (Brodick and Culzean) provided additional shelter for sensitive species, especially fruit. A fashion for growing exotic plants developed in the late 18th and 19th centuries, and both Brodick and Culzean have interesting collections of rhododendrons which are ideally suited to the west coast climate. The most remarkable consequence of this fashion, however, was not an unusual plant collection but the construction of an extraordinary garden house at Dunmore Park (no. 30) in the form of a huge pineapple. Other buildings associated with domestic sites from the middle ages to the 18th century are dovecots, and there are examples of late medieval beehive forms at Newark (no. 27), Crossraguel (no. 56) and Dunure (NS 252158), while at Westquarter (no. 31) there is a lectern type dating to the early 18th century.

At the lower end of the social scale, stone began to replace timber as the main building material in the 17th century. The change occurred first in the towns and particularly fine examples can be seen in Broad Street, Stirling (no. 15), and buildings on a slightly lesser scale can still be found in many of the medieval burghs (especially in Ayrshire).

At a later date, and most noticeably in Glasgow, the tenement became a common form of mass housing. Large numbers of these tenement blocks are still in use today, and we are fortunate to have The Tenement (no. 22) preserved as a reminder of how they looked in the past before they are all modernised. Lying midway between the extremes in the housing range come the substantial and comfortable Victorian and Edwardian middle class homes which abound in the more affluent suburbs of the towns. A somewhat unusual example of this type is open to the public in Helensburgh, where Charles Rennie Mackintosh's finest domestic commission, Hill House (no. 20), is now owned by the National Trust.

outside stair placed at the rear of the building. The National Trust have furnished it in the style of the late 18th century, and the upper room contains a collection of Burns memorabilia.

About 200 m north-north-east of the Bachelors' Club, there is an unusual motte (NS 432273) with two baileys.

19* Burns Cottage, Alloway, South Ayrshire

c AD 1730.

NS 334185. Burns Cottage and the attached Burns Museum are situated on the W side of the B 7024 at the N end of Alloway. The museum car park lies about 100 m to the S and is entered from Greenfield Avenue.

Bachelors' Club, Tarbolton (Left)

18* The Bachelors' Club, Tarbolton, South Ayrshire

17th century.

NS 431271. The Bachelors' Club lies in the centre of Tarbolton and is well signposted from Montgomerie Street (B 750).

NTS.

Like Souter Johnnie's House (no. 20), the Bachelors' Club owes its preservation to its association with Robert Burns. It was here, in the upper room, that Burns and his friends held the meetings of the Bachelors' Club in the early 1780s. The building itself is also of considerable interest, dating back about a century before the formation of the Bachelors' Club. It is of two storeys with harled and whitewashed walls and a thatched roof. The lower floor is divided into two apartments, while the upper is a single large room reached by an

The cottage in which Robert Burns was born (1757) has fortunately been preserved since the 1820s as a shrine to the poet, and consequently it has survived as one of Ayrshire's best remaining examples of early 18th-century rural vernacular architecture. Despite considerable alteration over the years and the ravages of fire, the house retains the character of the period and is furnished with contemporary fittings.

The cottage is of a single storey with reed thatch and, if Burns' father's description of it as 'an auld clay biggin' is correct, the walls may well be built substantially of clay; the latter are now harled and whitewashed—essential precautions if clay walls are to survive. Like many Scottish houses,

Burns Cottage, Alloway: about 1880

Bachelors' Club, Tarbolton: the kitchen (Left)

Burns Cottage, Alloway: about 1920

particularly those in towns, the cottage opens directly on to the road with no front garden (a medieval legacy—front gardens were prohibited in case they were used for dumping rubbish), and the front wall is gently bowed to follow the line of the road. Inside, the accommodation is divided into two sections (the but and ben) with the kitchen and living quarters at one end and the byre at the other. Little of the Burns family furniture remains; the box bed may be an exception, but the interior has been fitted out with 18th and 19th-century pieces, which give a good impression of the living conditions of a reasonably well-off farming family of the period.

While in Alloway the following are also worth visiting: Alloway Kirk (NS 331180); Old Bridge of Doon (NS 332178); Burns Monument (NS 332179); Burns Heritage Centre (NS 334180).

Hill House, Helensburgh
(Right)

20* Hill House, Upper Colquhoun Street, Helensburgh, Argyll and Bute

AD 1902-4.

NS 300838. From the A 814 in the centre of Helensburgh turn up Sinclair Street, climb the hill, turn left into Kennedy Drive and then right into Upper Colquhoun Street. Hill House is then on the right.

NTS.

The appropriately named Hill House stands above Helensburgh and commands extensive views to the south over the Firth of Clyde. It was Charles Rennie Mackintosh's major domestic commission, and the house along with most of its original furniture and fittings are now in the care of the National Trust for Scotland.

The house was built between 1902-4 for W W Blackie, the Glasgow publisher, and it was designed as a family home, but one in which Walter Blackie could also have privacy to entertain clients without disrupting the rest of the household.

From the exterior the house seems austere, even severe, with its plain harling and lack of ornament, but its interest is derived from the combination of traditional Scottish features with details that are

Hill House, Helensburgh: entrance to the staircase

clearly modern. Like Brodick Castle (no. 24), the interior is in complete contrast, containing a wealth of decorative detail, with the majority of the furniture and fittings also designed by Mackintosh. Each of the rooms is carefully composed, using simple overall designs to contrast with geometric patterns and highlighted by small splashes of colour.

parallel to the street, and has a kailyard (now a garden) at the rear. The building is of one storey with a thatched roof and wooden interior partitions. The National Trust for Scotland have restored and furnished the cottage.

While in Kirkoswald visit the ruined church and its fine collection of 18th-century tombstones.

Souter Johnnie's Cottage, Kirkoswald

21* Souter Johnnie's Cottage, Kirkoswald, South Ayrshire

AD 1785.

NS 240075. Souter Johnnie's Cottage lies on the E side of the A 77 in the centre of Kirkoswald.

NTS.

This typical late 18th-century village house was the home of John Davidson, immortalised as Souter Johnnie in Burns' poem Tam o'Shanter. Davidson was the village cobbler (in Scots, a souter) and he moved into this newly-built cottage in 1785. Like Burns' birthplace in Alloway (no. 19), the cottage fronts on to the main road with its long axis

**Tenement House,
Glasgow:
the parlour**

22* The Tenement House, Glasgow

19th-20th century.

*NS 581662. The Tenement House is at 145
Buccleuch Street, Garnethill. Viewing is by appointment
with NTS, Hutcheson's Hall, 158 Ingram Street,
Glasgow. Tel: 041-552 8391.*

From the outside, No. 145 Buccleuch Street is like
many thousands of other Glasgow tenements that
were built towards the end of the last century to
provide comfortable accommodation for the
growing numbers of lower middle class families.
But, unlike its neighbours, it has not been
modernised, and still remains much as it was in the
early decades of this century. This is not a recent
recreation of a 'twenties' interior but is the
untouched home, containing the personal effects of
an unremarkable Glasgow spinster, Miss Agnes
Toward, who lived here from 1911 until she entered
hospital in 1965. She died ten years later and in that
time her home remained untouched, until one of
her beneficiaries arrived, accompanied by his niece
Anna Davidson, to collect a bequest. Miss
Davidson was fascinated by the period piece flat,
bought it, and preserved the day to day
paraphernalia of Miss Toward's life.

Miss Davidson sold the flat to the National Trust
for Scotland, who recognised the unique
opportunity to conserve a complete household
which exemplified a way of life that was rapidly
disappearing.

By modern standards the flat is rather small,
comprising parlour, bedroom, kitchen and
bathroom, but by comparison with the cramped
housing conditions of much of Glasgow populace
in 1892, when the tenement was built, it was
spacious, and properties of this type would have
been much sought after.

**Tenement House,
Glasgow** (Right)

23* Weaver's Cottage, Kilbarchan, Renfrewshire

18th-19th century.

NS 401632. The Weaver's Cottage stands on the W side of The Cross (the square at the centre of Kilbarchan), between the junctions of Church Street and the appropriately named Shuttle Street; signposted.

NTS.

This carefully conserved cottage, dating from the early 18th century but with many later additions, is the last surviving example of a typical Renfrewshire weaver's cottage. It remained in use until 1940, and was acquired by the National Trust for Scotland in 1957; they have restored the interior to what it might have looked like in the mid 19th century and have turned it into a museum of the local handloom-weaving industry.

The rectangular stone-built cottage was erected in 1723 for John and Janet Bryden, who are commemorated in the inscription on the lintel over the front door. In the attic, preserved under a later roof structure, there are fragments of the original roof; it was of cruck construction and a layer of the turf thatch is still in position. The principal accommodation was on two floors; a weaving shop below with direct access to the street and garden, and the main living quarters on the upper floor which, because of the sloping nature of the site, could be entered from street level. Further sleeping space was provided by an attic which, over a period of time, was expanded to form a sizeable room.

The cottage has been refurnished with contemporary pieces, and some of the original fittings, particularly the box beds, have been restored. In the lower floor a handloom from a nearby cottage has been installed and weaving demonstrations are given on it. The garden retains some of its original features including a set of bee boles built into the wall which still contain straw skeps or hives.

The cottage-based handloom-weaving industry flourished in Kilbarchan from the late 17th century through to the 1880s when it was overtaken by power looms, but it continued producing specialist goods into the middle of the present century. Unlike the factory-based industry in nearby Paisley (famous for its shawls), the Kilbarchan cottage weavers produced a wide range of cloths and finished goods, and they were able to adapt their production to changes in fashion.

Weaver's Cottage, Kilbarachan (Left)

The Kitchen (Above)

24* Brodick Castle, Brodick, Arran

16th and 19th centuries.

NS 015378. Brodick Castle lies 1.8 km N of Brodick village and is well signposted from the A 841.

NTS.

Brodick Castle is reputed to be the oldest habitable property belonging to the National Trust for Scotland, and the earliest portions date to the 14th century. For the greater part of its history it was owned by the Hamilton family who acquired the estate and title of Earls of Arran in 1503. The castle and estate, which includes Goat Fell, passed to the

Brodick Castle, Arran

James Gillespie Graham, one of the most important Scots architects of the day, in what has now become known as the Scots Baronial style, and it marked a significant move away from the classical or Gothic styles that had been fashionable up till that date. Gillespie Graham's outwardly austere addition blends sympathetically with the earlier parts of the castle and contrasts with the richness of the interior decoration and furnishings, some of which were brought from the collection of William Beckford following his daughter's marriage to the 10th Duke of Hamilton.

National Trust in 1958 and it is renowned for its collection of art treasures and magnificent gardens.

Little of the castle's medieval work can now be identified and, as it stands today, the castle belongs to three main periods. A 16th-century tower-house forms the core of the building, to which Cromwell's troops added an extra wing and an artillery battery following their seizure of the island in 1652. The west wing, which forms the largest section of the castle, was not built until 1844; it was designed by

The gardens, which account for much of the attraction of Brodick, are laid out around the castle and include a number of garden buildings. To the north there is a walled garden of 18th-century date entered through fine wrought-iron gates, and in front of the castle a semi-formal area was laid out in the 1920s, which provides a splendid setting for the house. These terraces and beds give way gradually to woodland gardens with fine specimen trees and an important collection of rhododendrons which are in flower from February/March through to June.

Brodick Castle, Arran: elaborately decorated garden house

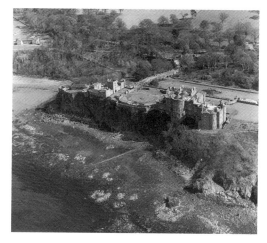

25* Culzean Castle, Maybole, South Ayrshire

18th and 19th centuries.

NS 250101. Culzean Castle lies on the coast about 7 km W of Maybole and is well signposted from the A 719 and A 77.

NTS.

Culzean (pronounced Cul-ain) is one of Scotland's greatest country houses and is renowned for its Adam interiors, magnificent gardens and Country Park. Formerly the principal seat of the Kennedy family, it was gifted to the National Trust for Scotland in 1945. Since then the house has been extensively restored both internally and externally; in 1969, the policies were created a Country Park with the Home Farm subsequently converted into a Park Centre containing an exhibition hall, restaurant, shop and a ranger office which provides guided walks through the park.

Until the mid 18th century Culzean was a simple late medieval tower-house, but from the 1760s to the 1780s the 9th and 10th Earls of Cassillis carried out a series of alterations which transformed the castle and the surrounding policies. The 9th Earl extended the accommodation, but the major work began in 1777 when the 10th Earl commissioned Robert Adam to remodel the house. Adam not only redesigned the building but was also responsible for the whole of the interior decoration, including much of the furniture and fittings. Since the National Trust took over the castle the Adam plasterwork and colour schemes have been faithfully restored, and Culzean is now a showpiece for Adam's work in Scotland. Building at the castle did not come to an end with Adam, and the growing demands for space by the family of the 14th Earl (the 3rd Marquis of Ailsa, 1848-1938) led to the reconstruction of the West Wing in 1879.

Surrounding the house there is a series of gardens set within the 565 acres of policies bequeathed by the 5th Marquis. References to 'pretty gardens . . . with excellent terraces' go back to the 1690s, and these doubtless formed the basis for the present formal garden known as the Fountain Court, to the south of the house. Specialised buildings such as the flamboyant Gothic Camellia House were added to cater for exotic plants, and on a more mundane

Culzean Castle: aerial view (Top Left)

The Old Eating Room (Above)

Culzean Castle: staircase (Left)

level the large walled kitchen garden was built to provide fruit and vegetables for the house. Around the more formal sections of the gardens, there are wilder areas containing specimen trees, shrubs and a lake (the Swan Pond) for waterfowl. Other structures worthy of note within the policies include a gas-producer house on the shore between the castle and the Home Farm, a system of caves beneath the castle which incorporate 16th century and later remains, and an early 19th-century gun battery.

Culzean Castle: Home Farm

Besides working on the house, Robert Adam also designed the Home Farm (1777); this unusual range of buildings is set around a courtyard which is entered through an arched gateway. These have been restored and now form the visitor centre for the Country Park; among the facilities is an exhibition hall which displays items relating to the house and estate, as well as explaining the agricultural improvements that were introduced to Ayrshire in the 18th and 19th centuries.

26* Kinneil House, Falkirk

16th and 17th centuries.

NS 981805. Entry by car to Kinneil Park is from the A 993, follow signposts for Kinneil Estate and Deangate Gardens; alternatively approach from the north along the A 904, follow the signpost, park at the foot of the cliff and walk up to the house via the Museum.

Historic Scotland.

Kinneil House: aerial view (Right)

Kinneil House forms the focal point of a large public park which contains a reconstruction of a

Roman fortlet (see no. 69), a museum set in a range of restored 18th-century farmbuildings, a ruined medieval church and part of an original James Watt steam engine. The principal attraction, however, is Kinneil House itself, which boasts a magnificent series of wall-paintings; it consists of two ranges of buildings set at right angles to one another, which were built and modified over a period of some two centuries.

The earliest building was a late medieval tower-house which lay on the site of the present west range, and all that can now be seen of it are a number of gun-loops incorporated in the rear wall of the later house. In 1553 the Earl of Arran added the present north range, known as the Palace, in order to provide more comfortable accommodation. Arran was obliged to spend the years 1564-9 in exile in France and, during this period, it appears that the tower-house was partly destroyed on the orders of the Earl of Morton. The house assumed its present form in 1670 when Anne, Duchess of Hamilton, began the reconstruction of what was by then a derelict group of buildings. Her remodelling consisted of building a rectangular block on the site of the earlier tower-house to which pavilions were added, the one on the north linking the new block to the Palace. On the south a further new wing was contemplated, which would have balanced the Palace, but it was never built, possibly because of difficulties with its foundations which lay across the line of the ditch of the Antonine Wall.

By the early part of this century the house was again abandoned, and during the course of

**Kinneil House:
mural paintings**

demolition in 1941 an important series of mural and ceiling paintings were uncovered in the Palace (the only part of the buildings now open to the public). Their discovery spared the house, and they are now on display in the first and second floors.

On the west side of the gully which flanks the house, there are the ruins of the medieval church of Kinneil, and part of an unusual medieval cross from the church is on display in the house.

To the south of the house is a building used by James Watt while he was trying to perfect a water-pump for one of the local coalmines. Outside the door there is the cylinder of a Watt engine which has been moved there from a local pit.

A small museum lies to the east of the house and it contains well-displayed collections of local Roman material and information relating to the industrial development of West Lothian.

Newark Castle: aerial view of the house and shipyards

27* Newark Castle, Inverclyde

15th-16th century.

NS 328745. From the A 8 on the E side of Port Glasgow follow the signposts towards the castle.

Historic Scotland.

A setting amidst the shipyards of Port Glasgow may seem a somewhat incongruous background for one of southern Scotland's finest 16th-century houses. In one way, however, it is quite fitting, as in 1668 the house and its surrounding land were sold to the magistrates of Glasgow for the express purpose of founding a harbour for the city merchants, and it was imaginatively christened New-Port Glasgow.

Newark Castle

The house consists of three elements disposed around three sides of a courtyard, with the 16th-century block on the north linking two earlier wings; the fourth side is now open, but at one time it was closed off by a curtain wall. The earliest part of the house is a 15th-century rectangular tower which forms the east wing. Facing it, on the opposite side of the courtyard, is the mid 16th-century gateway which, like that at Crossraguel Abbey (no. 56), provided both a fortified entrance to the courtyard and a tower with residential apartments above.

The principal interest of the house, however, lies in the commanding late 16th-century range that forms the north side of the courtyard. It is entered from the east, opposite the gatehouse, and above the entrance there is a panel bearing the date 1597 and the monogram of the owner, Sir Patrick Maxwell, together with the inscription 'The blissings of God be herein'. The basement is taken up with domestic offices including the kitchen, buttery, stores and, to the south of the main entrance, a large bakehouse. The greater part of the first floor is occupied by a large hall, built on the grand scale, with a magnificent fireplace on the north wall next to a turnpike stair. This staircase led to the private apartments and long gallery which were situated on the second floor. The external angles of this block are provided with corbelled angle-turrets which are complemented in the middle of the north wall by the semi-circular stair turret leading upwards from the hall. Set on the top of an angle-tower in the corner of a ruined wall to the north-east of the castle, there is a beehive dovecot similar to that at Crossraguel Abbey.

28 Provan Hall, Glasgow

16th and 18th centuries.

NS 667663. Provan Hall is situated in the East End of Glasgow, a little to the N of the M 8, and lies on the S side of Auchinlea Road between Garthamloch and Easterhouse.

NTS.

Now overlooked by a modern housing estate, Provan Hall is an example of a late medieval rural

Provan Hall, Glasgow

manor house which was probably intended to serve as a hunting lodge. By the beginning of this century it was semi-derelict, but in 1935 it was bought by a group of private individuals who restored the fabric and subsequently gave it to the National Trust for Scotland.

Although an earlier building may have stood on the site, the present house was probably erected in the later 16th century for Sir William Baillie, who acquired the land from Glasgow Cathedral following the Reformation. Originally, it comprised a house set on the north side of a walled courtyard which was entered through an arched gateway on the east. The house was rectangular on plan, with a circular stair tower projecting from the north-east angle; at a later date, an external stair rising from the courtyard was added to give direct access to the principal rooms on the first floor. An unusual feature of the gateway is the flight of steps leading from the courtyard to a look-out platform above the arch. In the 18th century the south side of the courtyard was filled in by a second house which, instead of fronting on to the courtyard, had its principal facade on the south, overlooking the valley of the Clyde.

29 Chatelherault, Garden Building, South Lanarkshire

18th century.

NS 736539. The entrance to Chatelherault is well signposted to the west of the A 72 about a mile and a quarter south-east of Hamilton, between Ferniegair and Allanton.

Although often described as the Duke of Hamilton's dog kennel, the grandiose garden building at Chatelherault was clearly not simply designed as accommodation for the ducal hounds. Standing on rising ground in the former deer park, it formed the focal point for the vista from the gallery of the now demolished Hamilton Palace (lying to the north in the Low Parks, east of Hamilton), and combined the functions of hunting lodge, banqueting suite, walled garden and kennels with that of a picturesque folly ornamenting the policies of the Hamilton estate.

Chatelherault was built in 1732 for the fifth Duke of Hamilton to designs by William Adam, and has been described as the last of the walled gardens of Scotland, a tradition of building that continued in

Chatelherault: the replanted parterre

Scotland long after it had died out elsewhere in Britain. The facade is divided into three parts: two flanking pavillions linked by a central portion behind which the kennels originally stood, with, at the rear, a formal walled garden. The east pavillion, which was plainly fitted out, provided accommodation for servants, possibly the kennel keeper and gardener, while the west pavillion formed the ducal suite containing a series of more elaborately decorated apartments culminating in a magnificent banqueting room on the upper floor, the plasterwork of which has been described as the finest of its date in Scotland.

Chatelherault owes its name to a French title bestowed in 1548 on James, Earl of Arran, an antecedant of the Dukes of Hamilton, by Henry II at the time of the betrothal of the Dauphin to Mary, Queen of Scots.

Following a period of neglect and vandalism, as well as sand quarrying to the north which threatened the survival of the building, Chatelherault has been restored and opened to the public. The east pavillion houses a small museum.

30 The Pineapple, Dunmore Park, Falkirk

AD 1761.

NS 888885. The Pineapple lies to the W of the A 905 a short distance NE of Airth.

Dunmore Pineapple: aerial view of the garden house and walled garden
(Right)

Cross-Section

The Dunmore Pineapple, which must rank as the most bizarre building in Scotland, has recently been saved from dereliction and is now available to let as holiday accommodation.

Originally, the Pineapple formed the focal point of the walled garden at Dunmore Park and was the centre-piece of a range of buildings that overlooked the gardens. Built in 1761 by an unknown architect, it was designed as a garden retreat and was flanked by stores and hothouses, in which pineapples may well have been grown. Its eccentric shape reflects the 18th-century interest in extravagant garden design and the craze for growing exotic flowers and fruit which required to be raised under artificial conditions.

31 Westquarter Dovecot, Redding, Falkirk

c early 18th century.

NS 913787. The dovecot lies on the S side of Dovecote Road, which is an E turning off Westquarter Avenue, and can be approached either from Polmont Road (A 803) or from Redding Road (B 805).

Historic Scotland.

This well-preserved lectern type dovecot now lies within a 1950s housing estate, but formerly it stood in the grounds of Westquarter House which was demolished to make way for the new houses. It is rectangular on plan with a perching course for the pigeons running right around the building above the level of the door. The side walls are crowstepped half way up the upper portion of the roof, and above this there is a parapet topped by scrolls and pilasters with ball finials at the corners. There are two rows of openings for the birds—a set of three above the door and a set of six halfway up the roof. Between the lower set and top of the doorway there is an heraldic panel dated 1647 which bears the initials of Sir William Livingstone of Westquarter and his wife Dame Helenore Livingstone, who were married in 1626. At first sight this would seem to suggest that the dovecot was of mid 17th-century date, but on architectural grounds this is unlikely, and it is probable that the panel either belonged to an earlier dovecot, or was brought from a different building altogether. In the interior there are the remains of several hundred nesting boxes, but the potence (a ladder which rotated around a central pivot, giving access to all the boxes) is missing, its position being marked by a circular socket in the centre of the floor.

For other examples of dovecots see Newark Castle (no. 27), Crossraguel Abbey (no. 56) and Dunure Castle (NS 252158).

Dunmore Pineapple: cross section (Left)

Westquarter, Dovecote

STONE CASTLES AND TOWER HOUSES

Bothwell Castle:
aerial view

The castles described in this section range in date from the 13th century, when the earlier earth-and-timber mottes began to be replaced by stone structures, through to the 18th century, after which there was little need for this type of static defence. Not all the mottes were translated into stone castles, as only the greater barons and king could afford the enormous costs of erecting a substantial masonry castle and the lesser nobility were obliged to opt for smaller structures such as hall- and tower-houses.

Throughout the medieval period two features dominated castle design: the need for a strong central point and the concept of an enclosing wall. Both elements hark back to the earlier mottes and ringworks of the Norman period, with the keep or donjon corresponding to the mottes central timber tower and the enclosure wall originating in the palisade surrounding the tower or forming the ringwork. In some cases castle plans were influenced equally by both features while in others one dominated the other. Loch Doon (no. 37), the earliest of the castles described in the guide, is a simple castle of enclosure, but at Bothwell (no. 33) there is both a massive enclosure wall and an impressive circular donjon. Entrances formed the weakest point of the defences and they were therefore the most heavily protected part of the enceinte. The elaborate, but never completed, gatehouse at Bothwell (no. 33) and the twin-towered gate at Stirling (no. 38) were one type of solution to the problem; another was to combine the function of the keep with that of the gatehouse, and a particularly fine example of this form can be seen at Doune (no. 35).

The introduction of artillery from about the 15th century onwards eventually rendered the complex defence systems of many castles obsolete, but some of the more important strongholds were modified to withstand artillery barrages. At Blackness (no. 32), the vulnerable landward wall was massively thickened and gun-loops inserted. Alterations such as these enabled many medieval castles to continue in use for several centuries, but in other cases entirely new castles were built, and at Craignethan (no. 34) Sir James Hamilton created one of the earliest of the new style castles on a fresh site using some of the principles of the new military architecture that he had learnt while on his travels in Italy.

From the 16th century there were rapid improvements in military architecture and the era of castles gave way to one of fortresses manned by professional armies. The number of these sites is comparatively low but the area is fortunate

Dumbarton Castle: the Governor's House

to contain the remodelled castles at Stirling (no. 38) and Dumbarton (no. 36) and the fragmentary remains of a Cromwellian fort in the centre of Ayr.

Tower-houses form the largest single group of medieval and post-medieval defensive sites to be found in the countryside. Their precise architectural origins are obscure, but in functional terms they replace the mottes of the lesser nobility as the focal points of estates and are frequently found in close associations with their Norman earthwork counterparts (see Clackmannan Tower, no. 40; Castle Campbell, no. 39). The earliest examples date to the 14th century (for instance Dundonald, no. 42), and are normally simple squares or oblongs on plan, rising to a height of three or four storeys. The groundfloor was used for storage and cooking, while the principal accommodation, the lord's hall, lay on the first floor with the private quarters above.

As the design of tower-houses developed, more elaborate plan-forms evolved, with the L-shaped tower being a common choice in the 16th and 17th centuries (Lochranza, no. 43; Clackmannan, no. 40), but even more enhanced plans are found as at Crookston (no. 41). Accommodation in tower-houses was severely restricted and, although the later towers were taller, this was not a satisfactory solution to the shortage of space. At Castle Campbell (no. 39) and Newark (no. 27) additional ranges were built and the courtyards enclosed by walls, creating a site halfway between a defensive medieval tower and a country house. This process of modification continued into the 18th and 19th centuries, long after tower-houses had ceased to be built, and consequently towers are often found at the core of what seem to be much later buildings (see Culzean no. 25). Another tower-house in an unlikely setting can be seen at Crossraguel (no. 56), where it is included within the buildings of the Abbey.

Dumbarton Castle: from the south side of the River Clyde

Blackness Castle: aerial view

32* Blackness Castle, Falkirk

15th to 19th centuries.

NT 055802. The castle is situated about 400 m NE of Blackness—follow the signposts from the centre of the village and park at the castle.

Historic Scotland.

This small, dour fortress occupies the tip of a promontory jutting out into the Forth and was designed to protect the port of Blackness which served as the harbour for the major late medieval royal centre at Linlithgow. Despite a long life as a stronghold, prison and ammunition dump, involving frequent rebuilding and strengthening of the fabric, the castle still retains important features from most of its major phases, and it serves as an excellent example of the development of fortifications from the mid 15th to late 19th centuries.

The earliest castle was built in the 1440s and comprised a ditch drawn across the neck of the promontory behind which there was a curtain wall surrounding a freestanding square tower, with a hall built against the south curtain wall. Much of this early fabric survives, although it has been masked by later additions. The ditch has been cleared out as part of the 20th-century restoration, and sections of the early crenellations can be seen fossilised halfway up the south tower. The primary function of the castle may have been defensive, but, like many other castles, Blackness served as a prison and the earliest historical reference to the castle, in 1449, records its use as a state prison. The castle continued to be used as a prison for the following 250 years, Cardinal Beaton, who was incarcerated there for about a month in 1543, being its most renowned prisoner.

Between 1537-42 the castle underwent a major programme of rebuilding in order to take account of the growing importance of artillery both in terms of defence and attack. This meant the provision of gun-holes and the massive thickening of the walls to withstand bombardment. At the same time the hall was heightened and took on the form of a tower in which it survives today. The remodelling of the castle was undertaken by Sir James Hamilton of Finnart, whose own castle at Craignethan (no. 34), built in the 1530s, exhibited similar innovations in the art of defence. Further stengthening occurred between 1542 and 1567 with the addition of a spur on the west guarding the newly positioned entrance. The castle was besieged

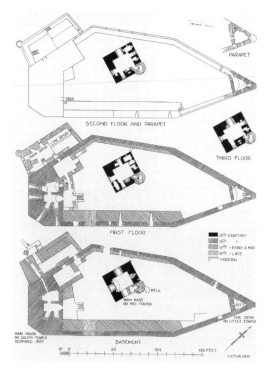

Blackness Castle: plans

Bothwell Castle: aerial view showing the castle lying in a bend of the Clyde

by Cromwell's army in 1650, and subsequent repairs to the south wall of the south tower can be seen as a patch of white stonework on the lower right of the tower.

In the 1870s the castle was converted to an ammunition store; the courtyard was covered, a cast-iron jetty built, and barracks erected outside the castle. After the fortress was handed over to the then Office of Works in 1912, most of these encumbrances were removed and the castle was restored to its present condition.

33* Bothwell Castle, South Lanarkshire

13th to 16th centuries.

NS 688593. Access to the castle is via the Bothwell road (B 7071) at the S end of Uddingston; signposted.

Historic Scotland.

The castle at Bothwell has been described by Douglas Simpson as 'among the foremost secular structures of the Middle Ages in Scotland', and, despite its ruined state, it still remains one of the most imposing of Scotland's earlier medieval castles. Originally planned by Walter de Moravia (Moray), who acquired the estate in 1242, it was laid out on a grand scale but was apparently only partially completed before the outbreak of the Wars of Independence (1296-1357) when it was twice besieged and deliberately dismantled in order to deny it to the English. In 1337, after demolition for a second time, the castle appears to have been abandoned until about 1362. It was then acquired by Archibald 'the Grim', 3rd Earl of Douglas who initiated an extensive programme of rebuilding which continued into the early 15th century. In 1669 Bothwell again changed hands, this time passing to the 1st Earl of Forfar, who built a new house to the east and partially dismantled the castle to provide stone for the new building.

As originally conceived in the mid 13th century, the castle was to comprise a five-sided enceinte with circular angle-towers, a square side-tower, a stoutly defended gatehouse and, dominating the whole structure, a massive round keep or donjon. The more vulnerable east side had the added protection of large earthworks, the north arm of which hooked around the gateway forcing attackers to approach from the south-east, thus exposing themselves to flanking fire from the wall-head. Only the keep, south-east wing wall and angle-tower, however, were completed; the remainder rose little further than foundation level. The keep is a particularly fine example and rivals the best work in England and France.

It was not until the late 14th century that the enceinte was completed in stone, probably for Archibald the Grim. The sequence of building, deliberate demolition and rebuilding has made the interpretation of the fabric fraught with difficulty,

34* Craignethan Castle, South Lanarkshire

16th-17th century.

NS 815463. Craignethan Castle is well signposted from the M 74 and from the A 744 and A 72.

Historic Scotland.

The development of artillery in the later middle ages rendered the defences of many of the earlier castles obsolete, and expensive or difficult alterations were necessary in order to give them sufficient strength to withstand a determined attack. A more radical solution to this problem was to build from scratch on a new site, and this was the case at Craignethan where Sir James Hamilton of Finnart built a stronghold for the Hamilton family. Sir James was the illegitimate son of the 1st Earl of Arran, and after travelling on the continent he returned to play his part in family affairs. While in Italy he had observed the rapid development of new styles of artillery fortification and, once back in Scotland, put his new found knowledge to practical use (see also no. 32 for Sir James' alterations at Blackness Castle). Work on the castle

but recent excavation has helped to solve some of the outstanding problems, as well as bringing to light an important collection of medieval pottery. Many of the vessels were complete and show that, although the forms of the jugs and other pots are of types found in northern England, they were, in fact, produced locally.

Bothwell Castle: the great tower
(Left)

Craignethan Castle: aerial view of the tower and ditch

began in the 1530s, with major additions being made before 1579; after it had gone out of use as a defensive structure, a laird's house was built in the outer courtyard.

The choice of this particular site for the castle is curious, for although it occupies the tip of a steep-sided promontory with good natural defence on three sides, the remaining flank is overlooked by higher ground which gave any assailant considerable advantage. In the earliest phase, the castle comprised a large tower-house surrounded by a walled enclosure (the barmkin) with the added protection of a dry ditch drawn across the neck of the promontory. The design is essentially medieval in character, but two features point to the future. In the first place, the exposed west wall (now reduced to its foundations but its original proportions can be seen in a reconstruction drawing in the site museum) was built on a massive scale in order to withstand an artillery barrage. The most novel feature of the plan, however, was the construction of a caponier at the south end of the ditch. This device, probably first seen by Sir James during his travels in Italy, was cunningly concealed in the base of the deep ditch and provided a stronghold from which the defenders could rake the length of the ditch with small-arms fire (for another example see Stirling Castle, no. 38). Soon after the construction of the early work the castle was extended by the addition of a walled courtyard attached to the outer side of the ditch.

**Doune Castle:
aerial view** (Right)

**Craignethan
Castle:

the caponier**

Craignethan's role as a defensive work ended in 1579 when it was partially demolished following the disgrace of the Hamilton family. In 1659 it was

bought by the Convenantor, Andrew Hay, who built a house in the south-west angle of the outer courtyard. The house is now occupied by the custodian, and in one of the outbuildings there is a small site exhibition and museum.

35 Doune Castle, Stirling

Late 14th century.

NN 728010. Follow the signposts to the castle from the Doune to Dunblane road (A 820).

Historic Scotland.

The castle occupies a naturally well-defended promontory above the confluence of the River Teith with the Ardoch Burn. Although the visitor's eye is instinctively drawn to the impressive and forbidding bulk of the masonry castle, there are outer defences comprising a suite of relatively slight earthworks (double ditches with medial bank) on the more vulnerable north side and a single bank and ditch on the south. Once the northern outworks have been crossed, the massive keep-gatehouse of the castle cuts across the neck of the promontory and lying behind it there is a courtyard protected by a curtain wall which still stands to its full height of 12 m.

Built shortly before 1400 for the Regent Albany (Governor of Scotland in the minority of James I), the design of the castle is unusual, combining simplicity with considerable defensive strength. It did not follow the contemporary fashion by relying

Doune Castle: the courtyard

on a defensive wall-head and projecting towers, but gained its strength from a high, simple curtain wall and an ingeniously planned keep-gatehouse. The latter was designed as two adjoining tower-houses, one for the lord's hall (on the east) and the other for the common hall; the two were not linked internally and both could have acted as separate redouts. The main entrance to the castle was through a simple passage under, but with no direct access to, the lord's hall. Thus the defences combined the advantages of the curtain-wall castle with those of the tower-house or keep.

Besides the keep-gatehouse, the courtyard contains a substantial kitchen block on the west and a range of lesser buildings on the east. The rear (south) wall of the castle is pierced by windows but there is no evidence to suggest that a range of buildings has been demolished along this wall, and it is more likely that they were never constructed.

The castle remained in use into the 18th century and during the '45, when it was falling into disrepair, it served as a prison. By the end of that century, however, it was roofless, but was restored between 1883 and 1886.

36 Dumbarton Castle, Dumbarton

14th to 18th centuries.

NS 400744. The castle lies on the shore of the Clyde a little to the S of the centre of Dumbarton and it is well signposted from the A 82 and A 814.

Historic Scotland.

The twin peaks of Dumbarton Rock (a volcanic plug similar in origin to Edinburgh and Stirling Castle Hills) rise dramatically from the north shore of the Clyde at its confluence with the River Leven to form a site of great natural strength, which is reputed to have the longest recorded history of any fortification in Britain. From at least the 5th century AD it served as the principal stronghold of the Britons of Strathclyde, thereafter it was a royal castle, and during the post-medieval period the castle was used as an artillery fortress guarding the approaches to Glasgow.

Little now survives of the early historic fortifications or of the urbs (town) mentioned by Bede, but excavations carried out by Professor Alcock in 1974-5 revealed the remains of a rampart

Dumbarton Castle: at the junction of the Rivers Clyde and Leven with the modern town of Dumbarton in the foreground

on the east peak, as well as finds of imported Mediterranean pottery and Merovingian glass. These, and the radiocarbon dates obtained from the rampart, tie in with the early documentary references to the site in the period AD 400-1000, when it was known to the Britons as Alcluith (Clyde Rock) and to the Irish annalists as Dun Breatann (Fort of the Britons). It is clear from the early references that the site was frequently attacked, and it owed its strategic significance to its proximity to the ford across the Clyde at Dumbuck (2 km to the east), which, until the channel was artificially deepened in recent times, was the lowest crossing point of the river.

Apart from sections of the Curtain Wall and the 14th-century Portcullis Arch, which guards the way up through the cleft between the two peaks, the medieval castle has been all but obliterated by the post-medieval fortifications. The advent of artillery necessitated a major reorganisation of the defences, and during the 16th and 17th centuries a series of batteries was built to cover the river and the approaches to the castle. Following the troubles of 1715 the defences were further improved with the addition of King George's Battery and the construction of the Governor's House (1735) at its rear. Minor alterations were made during the Napoleonic Wars, and the castle was last refortified during World War II when it was equipped with an anti-aircraft battery.

Loch Doon Castle
(Right)

37 Loch Doon Castle, East Ayrshire

13th century.

NX 484950. Loch Doon Castle is situated immediately W of the minor road that runs along the W shore of Loch Doon.

Historic Scotland.

Until 1935 Loch Doon Castle stood on an island in the centre of the loch, but in that year, following the decision to raise the level of the water, it was dismantled and partially reconstructed in its present position. Before demolition, the castle consisted of two elements, an early curtain wall and a later tower; the tower was not reconstructed in order to leave the more interesting early castle unencumbered.

Unlike the majority of the castles described in this volume, Loch Doon does not dominate the centre of a rich agricultural estate but is tucked away in a remote glen with its isolation exaggerated by its island setting. It belongs to a group of early stone castles, dating to the 13th century, known as castles of enclosure or curtain wall castles. The principal defence comprises a stout outer wall, which does not enclose a keep or donjon, the internal buildings being erected against the inner face of the curtain wall. Loch Doon Castle stands out as unusual in this group as it is polygonal, having eleven uneven sides, but it is likely that the shape was in part determined by the irregular nature of the surface of the island. The quality of the masonry is particularly high, being of fine ashlar with frequent use made of checked or rebated joints. Part of the interest of the castle lies in the completeness of

some of the minor architectural detail (particularly the entrances), which were doubtless spared from the ravages of the stone-robber by the inaccessability of the island site. The principal entrance to the castle was through a simple pointed archway protected by a portcullis and double-leaved doors which were kept closed by two draw-bars that run into the walls on either side of the gateway. A small postern gate is also well-preserved, and like the main gate, was secured by a drawbar.

Little is known of the history of the castle; the first reference to the site, presumably to the early castle, occurs in 1306 when it is described as a seat of the Earls of Carrick. During the reign of James V (1513-42), the castle is reported to have been burnt, and it is likely that the square tower was erected as part of the subsequent programme of reconstruction.

38* Stirling Castle, Stirling

15th to 18th centuries.

NS 790940. The castle lies at the top of Castle Hill and is well signposted from the town.

Historic Scotland.

Stirling Castle owed its importance in the medieval period to a combination of a crucial strategic position and a strongly defended natural fortress. Because it lay at the lowest bridging point of the River Forth, it commanded both major north-south and east-west land routes, and its possession was vital to anyone seeking military control of eastern Scotland.

Although the site of the castle has probably been occupied more or less continuously since prehistoric times, and is on record as an important

Stirling Castle: aerial view

Stirling Castle

Stirling Castle: reconstruction drawing of the King's presence chamber (Right)

Carved medallion of a fool from the presence chamber (Bottom right)

royal stronghold from the 12th century, the majority of the surviving remains date from the 16th to the 18th centuries. The late medieval castle lay around the highest part of the hill and comprised a massive curtain wall with square corner towers and a centrally placed twin-towered gatehouse (largely built about 1500). Within the enclosure formed by the curtain wall, there is a magnificent group of royal buildings reflecting the frequent use of the castle as the residence of the Scottish court in late medieval times. Principal among them are the Palace, Great Hall and Chapel Royal. The Great Hall is the earliest of these buildings, being contemporary with the curtain wall, and completed in the opening years of the 16th century. In form it is a typical medieval hall but built on the grand scale, outsizing Edward IV's Great Hall at Eltham and Henry VIII's at Hampton Court. Unfortunately, it was badly mutilated in the 18th century and is now being carefully restored. While the inspiration for the Great Hall looked back to the middle ages, the Palace, built only a generation later (between 1540-42), heralds the arrival in Scotland of the Renaissance style of architecture, and is witness to the renewed contacts between Scotland and France at this time. It is remarkable for the treatment of the exterior, particularly the sculpture; the interior, however, has been much altered and all that survives of the original fittings is a series of carved wooden medallions (known as the Stirling Heads) which once decorated the King's presence chamber. The Chapel Royal was built in 1594 for the baptism of Henry, the eldest son of James VI, and it is reputed that the best workmen were brought from all over the country to complete the work.

During the later 17th century considerable improvements were made to the north-west defences with the enclosure of the Nether Bailey, and within the castle the King's Old Buildings and the Grand Battery were erected. In the 18th century, following the Act of Union, an extensive programme of works was begun to improve the castle's defences. Between 1708-14 the outer defences were remodelled to take account of advances in artillery, and three large batteries were installed behind a broad ditch, the bottom of which was protected by a caponier (see also Craignethan Castle, no. 34). The castle remained an army barracks until 1958 when it passed into the care of the State. Historic Scotland is now in the process of making good many of the alterations carried out to the castle in the later 18th and 19th centuries, and a visitor centre and restaurant have been added.

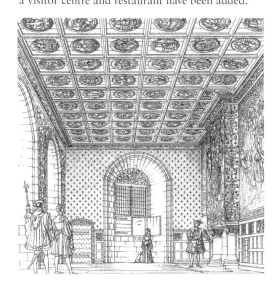

castle is a well-preserved oblong tower-house dating to the third quarter of the 15th century. It is of four principal storeys plus a garret, and rises within massive walls to an overhanging parapet. The internal arrangements are in keeping with most tower-houses and there is a hall occupying the first floor.

During the later 15th or early 16th century the residential accommodation was augmented by the construction of a south range, which consists of a series of vaulted cellars under a fine first-floor hall (cf Newark Castle, no. 27). In the late 16th or early 17th century a block was added on the east, linking the tower to the south range. An unusual feature of the east range is a double arched arcade, or loggia; this was a detail borrowed from the contemporary continental Renaissance style and was more suited to the sunny south than to the windy climate of Scotland. At about the same time that the east range was added, the courtyard was enclosed within a curtain wall and was provided with a gateway with a covered pend. To the south of the castle, and entered through a pend running beneath the south range, there is a small walled garden.

39* Castle Campbell, Dollar, Clackmannan

Late 15th-17th centuries.

NS 961992. From the centre of Dollar (A 91) follow the signposts to the castle.

Historic Scotland/NTS.

Castle Campbell is tucked away at the head of Dollar Glen and occupies the top of a promontory overlooking the confluence of the Burns of Sorrow and Care. From the 15th to the 17th century it served as the principal lowland seat of the Earls of Argyll; prior to 1490 it was known as Castle Glume, but in that year Colin Campbell, 1st Earl of Argyll, secured an act of Parliament changing its official name to Castle Campbell.

The present buildings date from the later 15th to the 17th century, but charter evidence suggests that there was an earlier castle on the site, and it is possible that the mound on which the tower stands is the remains of a motte. Like so many castles of the later middle ages, Castle Campbell developed from a relatively simple tower-house to a more complex design. The earliest section of the present

**Castle Campbell:
drawing of the
hall (Billings)**

Castle Campbell: aerial view

40 Clackmannan Tower, Clackmannan

14th-17th centuries.

NS 906919. Follow the signpost from the A 907 to the centre of Clackmannan and park by the Tolbooth. Walk up the High Street and through the gate at the W end into the field in which the tower stands.

Historic Scotland.

Clackmannan Tower: from the south-west

The well-preserved tower-house at Clackmannan stands on the crest of a ridge a short distance to the west of the medieval burgh, and it overlooks the town in much the same way as do the castles of Edinburgh and Stirling. The site first comes on record in 1365 when David II granted certain lands in the Sheriffdom of Clackmannan to Robert de Bruce, and it remained in the hands of the same family until 1772, although by that date the tower itself had been abandoned in favour of a more modern mansion house.

As might be expected, the building shows signs of several phases of construction, evolving from a simple rectangular tower to a more complex tower-house over a period of three hundred years, and there is some evidence to suggest that the stone structure may have superseded an earlier earthwork castle. The oldest section visible is to be found in the lower half of the north side; it forms part of a rectangular tower dating to the late 14th century, and was presumably built soon after the grant of the land to Robert de Bruce. In the following century the tower was heightened and wing added on the south, thus converting it to a conventional L-plan tower-house with the re-entrant angle situated on the south-west. The original entrance to the L-plan tower lay on the west, in the re-entrant, but, in the 16th or 17th century, it was replaced by the present entrance on the east. This was subsequently ornamented by the fine Renaissance archway that can still be seen today, and at approximately the same time, a belfry was added to the caphouse at the top of the turnpike stair. Outside the tower-house a walled forecourt was built in the 17th century, and a view in 1758 shows a ditch surrounding the tower which still survived in part as late as 1795.

41* Crookston Castle, Glasgow

12th and 15th centuries.

NS 525627. From the A 754 follow the signpost by turning into the Pollock housing estate. After about 100 m turn half left into a service road that flanks the Pollock road, follow it round to the left and park. The castle lies on top of the knoll to the right, and its entrance lies at the W end.

Historic Scotland/NTS.

Crookston Castle is situated on the top of a hogbacked knoll which offers a magnificent prospect over the Clyde to the higher ground beyond, and it is protected on the north by a steep drop down to the Leven Water. The defences belong to two main periods, a ringwork of 12th-century date and a later medieval tower-house of unusual design.

The castle takes its name from Sir Robert Croc of Neilston who held the lands of the manor in the latter part of the 12th century, and it is to this period that the earthwork defences probably belong. Although the site has in the past been described as the remains of a motte and bailey castle, excavation has shown that there is no evidence for the existence of a motte, and the earlier medieval defences are best described as a ringwork. The enclosed area is roughly oval on plan, measuring 80 m by 45 m within a broad ditch accompanied by a counterscarp bank. There is little sign of an inner rampart or stone wall, and a timber palisade probably provided sufficient defence. The single entrance lay on the west, under the modern track, and the interior buildings, like the palisade, are likely to have been entirely of timber.

The tower-house, which is of early 15th-century date, is of unusual plan and finds few parallels elsewhere in Scotland. Before deliberate partial demolition in the late 15th century, it consisted of a central rectangular block with four projecting angle-towers. Only the north-east and south-east towers now survive, giving the castle an unbalanced and ungainly appearance, although originally it must have been a handsome, if not formidable looking building. The principal accommodation lay in the central block, with the ground floor

Crookston Castle

occupied by a barrel-vaulted cellar, a large hall on the first floor and a solar above the hall; the angle-towers contained smaller apartments and the service rooms. The design of the castle and the masonry are of a high order and some of the work has been likened to that at Borthwick Castle, Midlothian.

Dundonald Castle: photograph taken about 1897

The castle was besieged in 1489 and the renowned cannon known as Mons Meg (now preserved in Edinburgh Castle) was dragged from Edinburgh to take part in the assault. Following the capture and slighting of the castle, it was re-occupied and partially restored, but before the end of the 16th century it seems to have been deserted.

42 Dundonald Castle, South Ayrshire

13th–15th centuries.

NS 363345. From the centre of Dundonald (junction of B 730 and B 750), take the signposted footpath to the top of Castle Hill.

Historic Scotland.

As it stands today, the tower-house at Dundonald is largely a work of the 14th century, but it incorporates part of an earlier castle built in the preceding century which, like that at Bothwell (no. 33), was partly demolished during the Wars of Independence in order to prevent it falling into the hands of the English army. Recent excavation has

Dundonald Castle: aerial view

discovered traces of hitherto unsuspected phases of construction, including a vitrified rampart round the top of the hill.

The early castle was an example of the keep-gatehouse type, with two semicircular towers projecting from the front of the main block flanking a centrally placed gateway which gave access to a rear courtyard. The south tower has been removed, but the base of the north tower can still be seen emerging from beneath the later stonework. Few other traces of the 13th-century castle can be identified.

Following his accession to the throne in 1371, Robert II had Dundonald rebuilt, converting the original gatehouse to an early form of tower-house. The front wall was reconstructed, largely removing the earlier towers; the central gateway was blocked and the main entrance was moved to the opposite side of the building. During the 15th century a new wing was added on the south and a barmkin built on the east. Robert's position as king and head of the House of Stewart was commemorated by a row of shields on the west wall which bear the royal arms and those of Stewart.

Internally, accommodation was provided on three storeys; a wooden floor/ceiling (now missing) separated the ground and first floors, but both the first and second floors are vaulted in stone. The hall lay on the second floor and was on a grand scale as befitting a royal castle, and an unusual feature is the ribbing on the roof vault. The castle was occupied until the 17th century, after which it fell into decay, and it is currently undergoing restoration.

43 Lochranza Castle, Arran

13th or 14th century to 16th century.

NR 933506. Lochranza Castle is situated on a gravel spit which projects from the SW shore of Lochranza, and it is approached by a side-road off the A 841. The signpost at the foot of the side-road gives the address of the castle key-holder.

Historic Scotland.

This outwardly simple and gaunt-looking ruined tower-house hides, within its walls, a surprise which gives added interest to what would otherwise be a comparatively run-of-the-mill tower. Until recently it was thought to be a 16th-century tower-house of typical L-shaped plan, but more detailed analysis of the fabric by Stewart Cruden suggested that incorporated within the 16th-century work there was a much earlier and more interesting building. Subsequent restoration of the castle confirmed Cruden's interpretation, and it is now clear that Lochranza Castle began life as a hall-house of the late 13th to mid 14th century.

Hall-houses are comparatively rare, the majority having been destroyed or, as in the case of Lochranza, incorporated into later buildings. They comprise small, compact buildings characteristically used by the lesser nobility whose finances could not extend to the construction of larger castles. In many ways they are the forerunner of tower-houses but they were never designed to reach the height of towers, and the principal accommodation was normally arranged on two floors, the lower being used for storage, while the upper floor contained the lord's hall. They are commonly equated with the English fortified manor house, and in a Scottish context they should be compared with early tower-houses such as Dundonald Castle, no. 42. The early features at Lochranza which led Cruden to propose the existence of the hall-house are a blocked doorway on the north-east wall, which gave direct access to the lord's hall, a number of long arrow-slits and several narrow windows with wide-splayed jambs and wide internal openings.

In the 16th century the hall-house was heightened to turn it into a conventional tower-house and crenellations were added. The internal arrangements were also considerably modified, with the principal entrance being moved to the middle of the south-west wall so that it would be overlooked by the wing that formed the foot on the L-plan.

Lochranza Castle, Arran

MOATED SITES AND EARTHWORK CASTLES

Dinvin Motte

Moated sites, sometimes also referred to as moated homesteads, form a small group of medieval earthworks about which comparatively little is known. Unlike the major series of early medieval mottes and ring-works, the moated sites probably belong to the later medieval period and may date to the 14th century. Their function and purpose are obscure, and it is possible that they filled a variety of needs. Many lie in remote areas, far removed from centres of population or from what would have been good agricultural land during the medieval period, and it is possible that some, Ballangrew (no. 44) and Peel of Gartfarren (no. 45) included, served as hunting lodges for the nobility and clergy, and can be compared to the 16th-century hunting lodge at Provan Hall, Glasgow (no. 28).

The introduction of feudal systems of land tenure during the 12th and 13th centuries was accompanied by the construction of new types of military fortifications. The best known of these are the mottes, or castle mounds, but other forms such as the ring-work have also been recorded.

Mottes vary considerably in shape and size ranging from the classic circular 'pudding basin' type, of which Carnwath (no. 47) is a characteristic example, to oblong or square mounds as seen at Sir John de Graham's Castle (no. 51). In some cases natural mounds were scarped to form the motte (eg Balfron, no. 52), while in others material for the mound was scooped up from a surrounding ditch. The ditch, however, also served as an integral part of the defences and at some mottes a second ditch was dug to give additional protection (Dinvin, no. 49; Balfron, no. 52; Dowhill, no. 50). The top of the motte would have been surrounded by a timber wall, or palisade, enclosing a wooden tower which was reached from the base of the mound by a flying bridge. Space on the summit was severely restricted and many mottes are accompanied by a bailey which provided room for ancillary buildings. Only one of the sites described here (Abington, no. 46) has the remains of a bailey, but it is possible that others were built solely of timber and, unlike Abington, did not have any form of embanked outwork.

Mottes are by far the most numerous of the earthwork castles but there are also a few examples of the other principal form, the ring-work. The best preserved is at Crookston (no. 41), where the later tower is surrounded by the remains of a substantial oval enclosure comprising a ditch and counterscarp bank within which there would originally have been a timber palisade. Inside the enclosure there would probably have been a hall, or tower, for the lord as well as a range of ancillary buildings, the whole complex closely resembling the arrangements at a motte-and-bailey castle.

There is little documentary evidence describing the details of the Norman settlement, but in the area of Upper Clydesdale enough has survived to show that the land was given by the Crown (probably David I) and settled by a group of Flemings who came to exploit the sheep-runs of the Lanark hills. These estates coincided with the newly created parishes, and there is a neat relationship of one motte per parish for part of this area. Unlike the situation often seen in England, the mottes in west central Scotland frequently lie at some remove from the medieval parish church and the village (eg Carnwath and Abington), and only at Biggar are all three found close together. It is not known for certain how long the mottes continued to be occupied, and it is likely that the timberwork may have been replaced on several occasions. At Roberton (NS 940271), one of the few mottes to have been excavated, pottery finds indicate that it may have remained in use at least as late as the 14th century, and so some of the mottes could have been succeeded directly by early tower-houses.

**Ballangrew,
medieval
earthwork**

44 Ballangrew, Moated Homestead, Stirling

14th-15th centuries.

NS 617988. From the Arnprior to Port of Menteith Road (B 8034), take the road to Ballangrew and park at the farmsteading. Follow the track through the farm and cross the fields towards the rougher ground on which the site is situated.

The well-preserved moated site at Ballangrew now lies on the north-west margin of Flanders Moss, close to agricultural land, but in medieval times, before a phase of extensive land reclamation in the 18th and early 19th centuries, it probably stood deep in the confines of the Moss and may have served as a hunting lodge.

Trapezoidal on plan, the central platform measures 23 m by 21 m within a broad water-filled ditch up to 8 m across which from the outset was probably intended to be wet. There is a slight indication of an inner bank on the south, but the bulk of the material from the ditch has been placed on its outer

lip to create a bank up to 1 m in height. Access to the interior must have been via a wooden bridge as there is no sign of a causeway across the ditch. In the 18th and early 19th centuries various objects of late bronze age to Roman date are reported to have been found in the interior, but it is likely that they were found nearby.

45 Peel of Gartfarren, Moated Homestead, Stirling

14th-15th century.

NS 536953. The site lies in a pasture field to the E of the A 81 about 100 m N of a bridge over a stream. Parking is difficult on the main road but it is possible to get at least one car off the road at a gateway directly opposite the site.

The Peel of Gartfarren is one of the best-preserved and most accessible examples of a moated homestead to be found in central Scotland. Like its near neighbour Ballangrew (no. 44), it is trapezoidal on plan and is defended by a relatively low inner rampart with a characteristic broad, flat-bottomed ditch accompanied by a low outer, or counterscarp, bank. Although the ditch is now dry, it may originally have been filled with water, and there are faint traces of what may be a feeder channel (marked by juncus rushes) leading from a small stream on the south towards the south-west angle of the ditch. The entrance is on the west, facing the road, and is marked by a gap in the rampart and a corresponding causeway across the ditch. The south section of the rampart has been extensively robbed, and on the south-west there are clear traces of where the carts have been brought into the site to carry away the stones. On the other three sides of the enclosure, there is a capping of stones on the crest of the rampart, suggesting that at some time a wall had been built on top of it, but it is not clear whether this is an original feature. In the north-east angle of the interior, there are the foundations of a rectangular building which is probably of comparatively recent date as the medieval buildings are more likely to have been of timber.

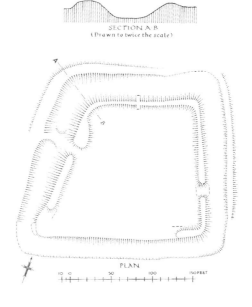

Peel of Gartfarren, moated homestead

Motte-and-bailey castle, Abington

46 Abington, Motte and Bailey, South Lanarkshire

12th century.

NS 932249. This castle is situated immediately E of the A 73 and about 150 m N of the junction with the minor road leading to Abington village. From a distance, the motte can easily be distinguished by the modern memorial stone which crowns its summit.

The motte at Abington is the only earthwork castle in upper Clydesdale to retain its outer bailey. The site has been carefully chosen to make maximum use of natural defences with, on the south-east, a steep drop of some 10 m down to the Clyde and a lesser stream protecting the south-west flank. The motte is tucked into the angle between the two water courses and is defended on the north and east by a ditch 10 m broad and 1.5 m deep. The oval mound rises to a height 2 m above the interior of the bailey and its summit measures 20 m by 12 m. There is no causeway across the ditch, and the timber tower that once crowned the mound must have been reached by a wooden bridge. The bailey lies to the north; it is irregular on plan, measuring a maximum of 80 m by 58 m within an earthen rampart accompanied by an external ditch. A modern track breaches the rampart on the north, but the original entrance is probably represented by a 4 m wide gap on the south-west.

The estate associated with the motte probably corresponded with the bounds of the parish of Crawfordjohn, within which it lies, and John of Crawford appears as a witness on a charter of lands in Lesmahagow between the years 1147 and 1164.

47 Carnwath, Motte, South Lanarkshire

12th century.

NS 974466. The motte is situated at the W end of the town and lies to the N of the A 70 in the middle of the golfcourse. Apply at the clubhouse, to the S of the main road, for permission to visit.

The motte at Carnwath, more correctly referred to as Libberton Motte as it originally lay in that parish, is the most impressive Norman earthwork to survive in Lanarkshire and can be viewed with advantage from the Carnwath-Carstairs road (A 70). It is a classic 'pudding basin' mound, circular on plan and rising with steep sides (now unfortunately planted with trees) to a level top, and surrounded by a ditch. For such a massive

Motte, Carnwath

earthwork (9 m in height), the summit area is surprisingly small, measuring a meagre 13.5 m in diameter, only marginally larger than the comparatively slight motte at Coulter (no. 46).

The motte may have been built for William de Sommerville (died 1160), who came from Yorkshire to Libberton at the invitation of David I.

48 Coulter, Motte, South Lanarkshire

12th century.

NT 018362. From the Biggar-Lanark road (A 72), follow the signpost along a minor road immediately E of Wolf Clyde bridge over the River Clyde. The motte lies on the NE side of the road 90 m N W of the bridge.

Historic Scotland.

This motte, like that at Abington (no. 46), overlooks the River Clyde but here all trace of its surrounding ditch and any associated earthworks have been removed by agriculture and modern development. The roughly circular mound measures about 12 m in diameter at the summit and it rises to a height of 2.5 m above the surrounding ground.

The earliest reference to a Norman noble in the parish is to an Alexander of Cutir who is on record as a witness to Charles of Maldoven, earl of Lennox, some time between 1225 and 1270, but it is likely that the castle was built at least one generation earlier in the preceding century.

49 Dinvin, Motte, South Ayrshire

12th century.

NX 200931. This motte is situated on the crest of a knoll 250 m NNE of the Girvan-Pinwherry road (A 714). Park close to the end of the road to Fardendew and follow a track on the opposite (N) side of the main road for a short distance before striking up the hill to the motte.

The motte at Dinvin is the most striking and best-preserved medieval earthwork in southern Scotland. It is built on a massive scale and far surpasses the other mottes to be found nearby. The outer defences consist of two large U-shaped ditches accompanied by external banks, the crests of which are up to 4 m above the bottoms of the ditches. At the centre, and making maximum use of the slope of the hill, the oval mound rises to a height of 4 m above the bottom of the inner ditch and measures 28 m by 19 m. Instead of the more usual flying bridge, the motte was entered via a ramp from the east, approached by a causeway which leads somewhat obliquely through the ditches and banks. For such a massively defended site, the internal area is comparatively small and it is disappointing that the motte is not accompanied by any trace of a bailey. For many years the scale of the defences led scholars to believe that the site was of iron-age date, and such a view was reinforced by the very name Dinvin, with the Celtic element dun suggesting a fortified site.

50 Dowhill Mount, Motte, South Ayrshire

12th century.

NS 202029. Dowhill Mount lies on the E side of the Girvan-Turnberry road (A 77) about 400 m N of the alginate factory at Dibble. Park in the layby on the E side of the road and climb up the old cliff-line to the motte.

This motte is perched on the edge of the degraded cliff-line and, except on the west, is defended by two broad flat-bottomed ditches accompanied by external banks. The oval central mound measures 31 m by 24 m in diameter and the summit rises to a height of 4.5 m above the bottom of the inner ditch. There is no sign of a causeway across the ditches and access to the interior must have been by way of a timber bridge. An unusual feature of this site, and one for which it is difficult to find a parallel, is a stone-walled enclosure built on top of the mound. Roughly circular on plan, it measures 14 m in diameter within a wall spread to a thickness of 4.5 m and up to 1 m in height. As it is not placed on the edge of the summit, it is unlikely to be part of a defensive wall or rampart and, if it is contemporary with the use of the motte (which there is no reason to doubt), it may have formed part of the sub-structure of the central timber tower. It certainly has no gap for an entrance and this would be in keeping with a first-floor entry to the tower.

51 Sir John de Graham's Castle, Motte, Stirling

12th-13th century.

NS 681858. This motte lies in a forestry clearing overlooking the N end of the Carron Reservoir. Take the B 818 and park close to Smallburn, then walk the 200 m through a narrow clearing in the forest to the castle.

Sir John de Graham's Castle is a fine example of a relatively rare type of medieval earthwork—the square motte; moreover, instead of heaping up an artificial mound, a natural knoll was chosen and defended by a broad, flat-bottomed ditch, 11 m across and 3 m deep. The ditch is continuous and access to the castle must have been via a wooden bridge which probably lay on the north-east side. The central platform is almost square and measures 22.8 m by 23.4 m. To the north-east of the ditch there are traces of a lime-mortared wall and fragments of banks which suggest the positions of ancilliary buildings.

Traditionally, the site is thought to have been the residence of Sir John de Graham, who was killed at the battle of Falkirk in 1298, and whose memorial can be seen in the graveyard at Falkirk parish church (NS 887800). The castle, however, may be of earlier date, as it was probably the principal stronghold of the barony of Dundaff which is on record in 1237.

52 Woodend, Balfron, Motte, Stirling

12th century.

NS 555887. This motte is situated immediately S of the junction of two minor roads about 900 m E of the centre of Balfron.

Although this large motte is now covered by a conifer plantation, the trees are sufficiently widely spread not to obscure a view of the mound. The motte consists of a natural mound, about 3 m in height, the top of which has been levelled to provide an oval platform measuring 40 m by 34 m in diameter. The site was chosen for its natural strength, being defended on the south-west and east by natural gullies which unite on the south-east, and all that was required to complete this defence was to dig a ditch linking the heads of the two gullies. This artificial ditch has been partially filled in and its course overlain by a plantation bank that fringes the modern road.

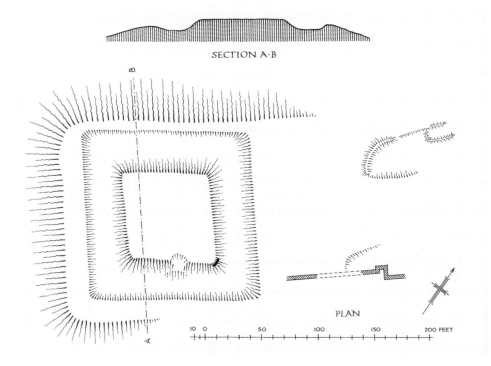

SECTION A·B

PLAN

Sir John de Graham's Castle, square motte

CATHEDRALS, ABBEYS AND CHURCHES

Despite liturgical and organisational changes brought about by the Reformation, which led to the neglect and decay of many fine buildings, the area still contains good representative examples of most facets of the medieval church, ranging from the great cathedrals and abbeys to the humbler parish churches. Of the latter comparatively few remain, but from the later medieval period the area is fortunate in having a series of collegiate churches which helps to fill the gap left by the small number of parish churches.

Church building all but ceased for about a century after the Reformation, and it was not until the 18th century that it resumed the proportions reached in the earlier period. Many of the medieval sites were abandoned in favour of more convenient locations, leaving the earlier churches and graveyards to decay. On the other hand, the growing towns with rich parishes were provided with fine churches, many of which are now suffering the same fate as their medieval counterparts as church attendances drop and populations move away from the 19th-century industrial centres. Once again all is not lost as the development of new towns has given a boost to church building sinc the Second World War (see no. 68).

Collegiate churches, two of which are described later (nos 60 and 62), were a late medieval development in which a patron (usually aristocratic) established a community of secular (ie non-monastic) clergy to perform the daily offices and to hold masses for the founders and their families. The buildings, as might be expected, were normally of some architectural pretensions and frequently contain the tombs of their founders (see no. 60).

For other examples of collegiate churches, see Biggar (NT 041378), Bothwell (NS 704586) and Carnwath (NS 975464).

St Bride's Church, Douglas: datestone

The later medieval obsession with death, inspired by the depradations of the plague, established a pattern of funerary memorials that was to last well into the present century. The earliest memorials, such as those at St Bride's Church, Douglas (no. 63), were aristocratic in origin, but in the following centuries the fashion worked its way through the entire social system. The Skelmorlie Aisle (no. 64) is an unusually elaborate 17th-century example, and by the early 18th-century a vigorous tradition of carved grave-markers had grown up in much of west central Scotland. Good collections of 18th-century tombstones can be seen in many of the older graveyards, particularly in Ayrshire (see Alloway Old Parish Church and Kirkoswald). In the 19th century the new rich, especially in the towns and cities, displayed their wealth by erecting grandiose memorials; one of the best collections can be seen in the Necropolis attached to the cathedral (no. 54) in Glasgow, and this rather vulgar exhibition should be contrasted with the more restrained style in the Church of the Holy Rude, Stirling (no. 11) and Dunblane Cathedral (no. 53).

Dunblane Cathedral: the cathedral and tower

53 Dunblane Cathedral, Stirling

12th-16th centuries.

NN 781013. The cathedral is situated N of the main street in Dunblane. Parking may be difficult in the town but there is a car park immediately to the N of the cathedral.

Historic Scotland.

Dunblane is an attractive small town regaining a quiet charm now that the main Stirling-Perth road has been diverted west of the town centre. On higher ground flanking the River Allan and at the head of the main street, the cathedral stands surrounded by a close-like grouping of buildings, some of which date back to the 17th century. From the 13th century the cathedral was the seat of the bishop of the diocese of Dunblane, which stretched from the Forth to Strathearn. Before that date the episcopal centre was probably at Muthill but, as a part of the reorganisation of the church in the early 13th century, Bishop Clement moved to Dunblane and oversaw the construction of a new cathedral. After the Reformation, the cathedral fell into decay; only the choir retained its roof and, like Paisley Abbey (no. 59), it was converted for use as the parish church. During the late 19th century the cathedral was restored by the renowned Scottish architect Sir R Rowand Anderson.

There has probably been a church at Dunblane since Early Christian times but all that survives from this early period are fragments of sculpture and a complete cross-slab of 9th or 10th-century date which are now situated in the north-west of the choir. The construction of the cathedral by Bishop Clement meant the demolition of the 12th century church, but its freestanding square bell-tower was incorporated, not quite at right-angles, into the south wall of the cathedral.

During the later middle ages the tower was progressively heightened and the two major building periods can readily be distinguished by changes in the colour of the stonework. Although work on the cathedral may have begun soon after the installation of Bishop Clement in 1233, the building was probably not completed until late in the century and modifications continued to be made up to the Reformation. Preserved within the

sanctuary and at the west end of the nave there are rare examples of medieval stalls; the fine modern choir-stalls were designed by the Scottish architect Sir Robert Lorimer.

The cathedral is surrounded by a burial-ground which contains an interesting collection of 18th and 19th century gravestones, and, immediately outside the burial-ground, the Friends of Dunblane Cathedral have restored a late medieval house for use as a museum.

54 Glasgow Cathedral

13th-15th centuries.

NS 602655. The cathedral is situated to the E of the present centre of the city. It is readily accessible by public transport and by car, but parking is rather limited.

Historic Scotland.

There has probably been an ecclesiastical establishment on the present site since Early Christian times. St Kentigern (popularly known as St Mungo) is reputed to have founded a church here in the late 6th or early 7th century, and later it served as the seat of the bishops of the Kingdom of Strathclyde. Glasgow retained its status following the absorption of the Kingdom of Strathclyde into that of Scotland, and the church underwent much

Dunblane Cathedral: the nave

Dunblane Cathedral: Pictish cross

**Glasgow
Cathedral**

**Detail of a lamp-
standard from the
cathedral** (Right)

The east end
(Below)

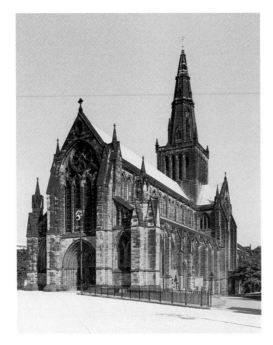

alteration until the present layout was established in the 13th century. Recent excavations have revealed traces of the 12th-century church and it is likely that many fragments have been incorporated into the present fabric.

As it stands today, the building is of a somewhat unusual design comprising a double church, with the lower church lying below the choir of the cathedral. The lower church was designed to hold the relics of St Kentigern, but no longer does so, as they were removed in the later middle ages. The upper church is rectangular with the nave divided from the choir by a stone pulpitum placed between transepts which do not project beyond the walls of the nave. The eastern part of the church was rebuilt under the direction of Bishop Bondington (1233-58), but on stylistic grounds it is clear that the nave was not completed until the next century as it incorporates work of 14th-century character. By the end of the 14th century the cathedral had assumed its present form; the only major addition was the erection of the Blacader Aisle on the south side of the church. This was began by Bishop Blacader (1483-1508), and was probably intended to house the Shrine of St Kentigern. Unfortunately it was never completed, only the lower portion being built. The west end of the medieval church was flanked by two towers, but these were removed in 1846. Preserved in the Lower Church there are a

number of medieval monuments, a collection of architectural fragments (many of which come from the 12th-century church), as well as the remains of the 13th-century Shrine of St Kentigern.

Close by the cathedral there is the Necropolis containing an impressive array of tombstones dating from the 18th and 19th centuries.

55* Cambuskenneth Abbey, Stirling

13th century.

NS 808939. From the A 907 turn into Ladysneuk Road and follow it to the Abbey.

Historic Scotland.

The ruins of this abbey, formerly known as the Abbey of St Mary of Stirling, lie in a bend of the Forth and are overlooked by the major medieval castle and town of Stirling. Founded in c 1147 by David I (c 1084-1153), the abbey was a daughter house of the French Augustinian monastery of St Nicholas at Arras and, because of its proximity to the royal castle at Stirling, it was the setting for a number of important historical events, which included meetings of Parliament in the 14th century and a visit by Edward I of England in 1303-4. During the Wars of Independence (1296-1357), the abbey suffered structural damage and was pillaged of much of its furniture and treasure. In 1559 the abbey was dissolved and the buildings were subsequently used as stone quarries for Stirling—some of the stone being removed to build Mar's Work (no. 13) and Cowane's Hospital (no. 14).

Although founded in the mid 12th century, the main period of construction did not take place until late in the following century when a cruciform church flanked on the south by a cloister, chapter-house and refectory were built. These have now been reduced to little more than their foundations, and much of what can be seen today is the result of reconstruction during the 19th century. In the course of excavations in 1865 what are believed to have been the coffins of James III (died 1488) and his queen, Margaret of Denmark, were found near the high altar. The royal remains were subsequently reburied at the expense of Queen Victoria, and the new tomb can be seen on the site of the former high altar.

The best-preserved, but heavily restored, part of the abbey is the bell-tower, which lies to the north-west of the church. It is the only surviving example from medieval Scotland of a free-standing belfry—a type of building more familiar in Italy. The tower was probably erected some time after the church and abbey buildings but its precise date of construction is unknown.

Glasgow Cathedral: the nave (Left)

Cambuskenneth Abbey: the bell-tower and the foundations of the abbey building

Crossraguel Abbey: aerial view

Detail of a medieval tomb (Right)

and its west angles) as the abbey was devastated during the Wars of Independence (1296-1357). In the following century the church was rebuilt, the cloister and Inner Court were erected and, during the 15th-century, as the wealth of the abbey increased, buildings were added around the South Court. Perhaps the most interesting of the 15th-century buildings are the small houses which occupy the south range of the South Court; such houses are relatively common in England but are only rarely found in Scotland. They were occupied either by members of the community or by retired clerics and laymen who wished to spend their old age within the security of a religious foundation; one such grant of corrody was made to Abbot Roger of Crossraguel who, in 1370, retired to the Abbey of Dunfermline.

56* Crossraguel Abbey, South Ayrshire

13th to 16th centuries.

NS 275083. Crossraguel Abbey is situated immediately S of the A 77 about 2 km SW of Maybole. It is signposted from the main road and a car park is provided adjacent to the abbey.

Historic Scotland.

This small Cluniac monastery (only ten monks are on record in the 15th century) was founded in the early 13th-century by Duncan, Earl of Carrick, and it was a daughter house of Paisley Abbey (no. 59). Now somewhat reduced by the ravages of time and the stone-robber, the abbey is an interesting example of a compact medieval monastery with a number of features of particular note.

As it stands today, the abbey consists of a church flanked by a cloister and a courtyard (The Inner Court), and, separating the two, there is a range of buildings which contains (from north to south) the sacristy, chapter house and treasury. To the south-east of the cloister there is a second courtyard (The South Court) which is flanked by buildings and a strongly defended gatehouse. Acting as sentinels to the whole complex there is a tower-house on the east and a beehive dovecot on the west.

Crossraguel Abbey: the abbey cloister (Right)

Although the earliest stone buildings were erected in the 13th century, little now remains from this period (the lower courses of the south church wall

Crossraguel's last regular abbot was William Kennedy (1520-47). During his abbacy the nave and choir of the church were divided by a stone wall and the tower-house, gatehouse and dovecot were added. The tower-house is an unusual feature for a monastery and, together with the gatehouse, may have been built to accommodate the Earl of Cassillis who, as a minor, stayed at Crossraguel for eleven years under the guardianship of his uncle, Abbot William.

57* Inchmahome Priory, Stirling

13th-14th centuries.

NN 574005. Inchmahome is an island in the Lake of Menteith and is served by a regular (free) ferry which plies from the Port of Mentieth. The ferry leaves from a jetty (where there is ample car-parking space) immediately W of the B 804 about 500 m S of its junction with the A 873.

Historic Scotland.

There are two islands in the Lake of Menteith; the smaller is occupied by the Castle of Inchtalla, while the larger houses the Priory of Inchmahome, which must be one of Scotland's most attractively sited monuments. The Augustinian Priory was founded in 1238 by Walter Comyn, 4th Earl of Menteith, but there may have been an Early Christian monastery on the island. All that remains to be seen of the latter establishment, however, is a rather poorly-carved slab preserved in the Chapter House. The Priory remained in ecclesiastical hands until the early 16th century when the land was leased to a lay family, after which it became, to all intents and purposes, the heritable property of the Erskines. Following the battle of Pinkie (1547), the young Queen Mary and her mother were lodged for safe-keeping with the monks at Inchmahome for three weeks, but by the end of that century the island had lost its religious community.

Although the Priory is now ruinous, enough survives to give a vivid picture of this compact religious house with its spacious church and conventual buildings ranged around the cloister. Building and remodelling continued over a long period, and this is particularly noticeable at the west end of the church where a square bell-tower was added in the late medieval period, and on the south of the cloisters where the foundations of an earlier range of buildings have been exposed. Some of the piers and the west doorway of the church show marked similarities to work at Dunblane Cathedral (no. 53), which was under construction at about the same time, and it is possible that some of the masons were involved in both projects. Originally there was a group of medieval grave-markers and effigies in the church but most have now been moved to the Chapter House for greater protection.

During the medieval period the monks cultivated parts of the island, and traces of field banks and other enclosures can still be seen; on the west of the island there is a small knot garden (cf the much more elaborate example at the King's Knot, Stirling, no. 16) which is traditionally, but probably erroneously, associated with Mary, Queen of Scots.

Tombstone of Sir John Drummond

Inchmahome Priory: aerial view

**Kilwinning Abbey:
aerial view**

at Glasgow Cathedral. The base of the south-west tower still survives, showing that it was entered from the nave through a pointed archway; the north-west tower stood until 1805 when it was struck by lightning and was subsequently replaced by the present bell-tower. Excavation, between 1961 and 1963, has demonstrated that the medieval work at the abbey was carried out in two stages. The earliest period belongs to the late 12th century, soon after the founding of the abbey, but construction appears to have ceased before either the west end of the church or the west claustral range had been completed. In the later period, dating to the 13th century, a more ambitious plan was envisaged; as in the earlier period, however, work stopped before the buildings were finished.

Little is known of the detailed history of the abbey as its chartulary has been lost but, by the middle of the 16th century, the abbey and its lands had passed into the hands of a commendator, and in 1591 the abbey itself was in ruins. Later, part of the church, probably the choir, was repaired and used as a Presbyterian church. This was taken down in 1775 and replaced by the present parish church.

58 Kilwinning Abbey, North Ayrshire

12th and 13th centuries.

NS 303432. The Abbey lies in the centre of Kilwinning and can be approached on foot along the pedestrianised main street or directly by car from the S.

Historic Scotland.

The fragmentary remains of this once important Tironensian abbey are situated in the burial-ground of the present parish church, and are currently undergoing consolidation. The abbey was founded about 1162 by Hugh de Moreville, possibly on the site of an earlier church, and it was colonised by monks from the major Tironensian abbey at Kelso, Roxburgh.

All that remains visible of the abbey church and its claustral buildings are parts of the south-west church tower, the south wall of the church (which incorporates an almost complete processional doorway leading from the nave to the cloisters), the gable of the south transept (rising to a height of some 27 m), and the doorway and side walls of the chapter house. Excavation in the 19th century, however, recovered much of the plan of the church and showed that, originally, it was of cross plan measuring 68.5 m in internal length by 19.8 m across the nave and 9.1 m across the chancel (now buried beneath the parish church). At the west end there were two projecting corner towers, like those

**Kilwinning Abbey:
processional
doorway** (Right)

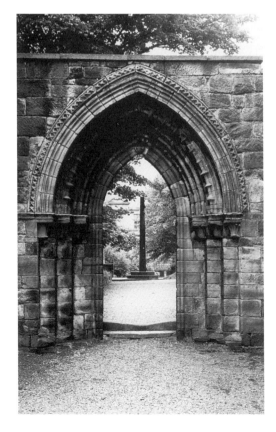

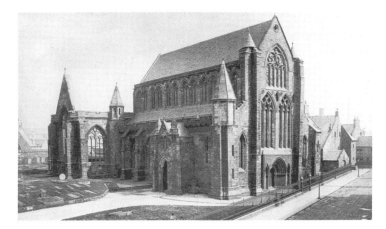

59* Paisley Abbey, Renfrewshire

12th to 14th centuries.

NS 485659. Paisley Abbey lies in the centre of Paisley on the E bank of the White Cart Water.

The Cluniac priory of Paisley (it was not raised to the rank of an abbey until 1245) was founded by Walter, son of Alan, steward of Scotland, about 1163, and it replaced an earlier Celtic monastery dedicated to St Mirin. Walter invited monks from Wenlock Abbey, in his native county of Shropshire, to colonise the priory and in 1169 Humbold, prior of Wenlock, came north bringing thirteen monks to establish the community.

Little of the 12th- to 13th-century church now survives; it was burnt by the English in 1307 during the Wars of Independence and appears to have been extensively damaged. Portions of early work can still be seen in the great west doorway, in the south wall of the nave and in the processional doorway leading from the nave to the cloisters.

Rebuilding began in the late 14th century but the greater part of the church belongs to a major period of reconstruction undertaken in the mid 15th century. It is of cross plan with a graceful aisled nave, an unusually long choir, and has a tower situated over the crossing. The principal feature of the choir is a decorated four-bayed sedilia (seats for the use of the clergy during the celebration of a mass), which lies at the east end of the south wall. Opening off the east wall of the south transept there is a side-chapel dedicated to the Celtic saint, St Mirin; erected in 1499, it contains a frieze below the east window filled with carved panels showing scenes from the saint's life. Such friezes must originally have formed a regular feature of interior decoration but few now remain, and the Paisley group represents a most fortunate survival. The chapel roof is also of interest as it is a double barrel-vault, a form of roofing more commonly encountered in tower-houses than in ecclesiastical architecture. In the centre of the chapel there is an ornamental medieval altar-tomb; it was found in fragments and reconstructed in 1817 and is thought to belong to Margery, daughter of Robert I. However, there is some doubt about the authenticity of the monument as it may have been

pieced together from fragments of more than one original structure. In the nave and transepts there are a number of medieval grave-slabs, but the most important stone monument in the abbey is the Early Christian cross from Barochan, Renfrew, which stands in the nave (described in detail below, no. 65). Only portions of the claustral buildings survive: at the Reformation parts of the south range were converted to domestic use by the Commendator and became known as The Place (Palace) of Paisley. During the early 19th century The Place fell into disrepair but it has subsequently been restored for use by the congregation.

Until the late 19th century much of the abbey church lay in ruins and only the nave was roofed; since then extensive restoration has been carried out and the whole of the church is now in use.

Paisley Abbey before reconstruction

Paisley Abbey drain

Castle Semple, collegiate church

Late medieval grave-slab (Below)

Lord Sempill's burial monument (Bottom)

60 Castle Semple, Collegiate Church, Renfrewshire

Early 16th century.

NS 375601. From the minor road linking Howood and Lochwinnoch, turn SW along the private road to Castle Semple, a short distance to the W of Brides Mill Bridge (NS 382609). Follow the track through Castle Semple farmsteading and park by the Church.

Historic Scotland.

This unusual collegiate church was founded in 1504 by John, Lord Sempill, in his grounds at Castle Semple, and it was endowed with a provost, six chaplains, two boys and a sacristan. The original building comprised an oblong church with a rectangular tower at the west end, but this simple plan was embellished following Lord Sempill's death on the field of Flodden in 1513 by the addition of a three-sided apse at the east end, which was designed to house his funerary monument. The two portions of the building differ considerably in style with the plain, rather austere treatment of the fabric in the west half contrasting with the more flamboyant decoration of the late Gothic tracery in the windows of the apse.

The interior of the building has been partially restored with the removal of two relatively recent partition walls and the replacement of some of the dressings around the windows. This allows the visitor an unrestricted view of the principal feature of the interior, the exuberant late Gothic burial monument of Lord Sempill, which lies at the east end of the north wall. His effigy, if it was ever added, is now missing, but this hardly detracts from the fine monument. To the left of the monument, the grave-slab of Gabriel Sempel, who died in 1587, has been placed against the wall. Around the doorway on the north wall and on the step leading to the dais at the east end, numerous mason's marks are still visible.

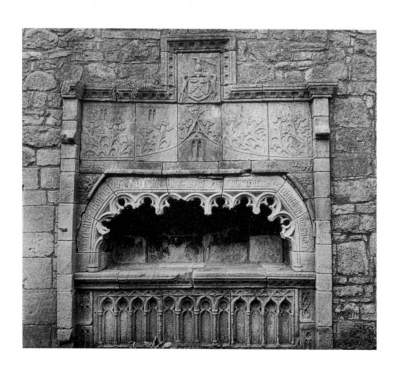

Lamington Church

61 Lamington Church, Romanesque Doorway, South Lanarkshire

12th century.

NS 978309. The church lies at the SW end of Lamington village, on the right-hand side of a minor road, about 150 m NW of its junction with the Biggar-Abington road (A 702).

Incorporated into the outer face of the north wall of the present church (built in 1721), there is an elaborate Romanesque doorway which is all that can now be seen of the original 12th-century Norman church dedicated to St Ninian.

The door mouldings are generally well preserved, particularly over the archway, but it is unfortunate that a pair of shafts which originally flanked the doorway has not survived and only their plain capitals remain. The mouldings are arranged in three orders and decorated in a typically bold Norman style. To give the illusion of greater height, the outer order has been ingeniously carved so that the spaces between the rings decrease from the caps towards the crown of the arch. An iron bar on the left hand side of the doorway is all that remains of the village jougs (iron shackles to restrain minor offenders, cf stocks). The churchyard still retains its roughly circular shape - indicative of its early date - and within it there is a good collection of 18th-century gravestones, as well as at least one of late 17th-century date.

The church and village of Lamington were founded by a Norman knight, Lambin Asa, who was in possession of the surrounding land by 1164, and what might be his motte lies 1.2 km to the east in a side valley below Lamington Hill (NS 992309).

Lamington Church: Romanesque doorway

Maybole, collegiate church

62 Maybole, Collegiate Church, South Ayrshire

14th to 17th centuries.

NS 301098. In the centre of Maybole take the road to Crosshill (B 7023), follow it for about 200 m before turning left into Abbey Street and the church lies a short distance on the right.

Historic Scotland.

The original church, dedicated to St Mary, was founded by Sir John Kennedy of Dunure in the early 1370s, and by 1382 it had been established as a collegiate church with endowments for one clerk and three chaplains. Its early foundation makes it one of the first collegiate churches in Scotland, and it marks the beginnings of a fashion that was to flourish in the following two centuries.

The present building, which has recently been restored, consists of the roofless remains of a rectangular church with a barrel-vaulted sacristy opening from the north wall. Although the original church was built in the late 14th century, the majority of the present fabric appears to be of 15th-century date but built in a deliberately archaic style. The earlier church was probably smaller than the present building and may have been extensively remodelled in the 15th century, with the only 14th-century details now visible being a narrow lancet window in the south wall and a nearby dressed corner. The fine south-west doorway is in imitation of 13th-century work and is surmounted by an armorial panel bearing the Kennedy arms. At the east end of the north wall there is a tomb-recess with a pointed arch-head which, like the south-west doorway, is decorated with dog-tooth ornament in a deliberately old-fashioned style. In the 17th century a burial-vault was added on the north side of the church for the laird of Culzean (No. 25); it has an elaborate doorway above which there is a large, but sadly rather decayed armorial panel bearing the arms of Kennedy impaled with those of an unknown family.

During the Reformation the house of the provost of the church, which stood close to the High Street, was the scene of a celebrated debate in 1561 between John Knox and Quentin Kennedy, abbot of Crossraguel.

63 St Bride's Church, Douglas, South Lanarkshire

14th to 16th centuries.

NS 835309. The church is situated in the centre of Douglas, to the N of Main Street which lies to the N of the Cumnock Road (A 70). Access to the burial-ground is signposted and a notice on the gate gives instructions for obtaining the key to the church.

Historic Scotland.

Although a church at Douglas is on record in the 12th century, the present building is pobably of late 14th-century date. It is in a much ruined condition

Maybole, collegiate church: doorway

with only the choir now roofed, and until the mid 19th century this too lay open to the elements but was covered during extensive restoration work carried out on behalf of Lord Home. The nave is missing but the shell of the south aisle survives, and from its east end rises the attractive octagonal bell-tower which was inserted in the 16th century.

The principal attraction of the church, however, lies in the interior, where there is an important series of medieval grave-effigies and burial-monuments, most of which are associated with the Douglas family who have been major local landowners from the medieval period to the present day. The oldest datable monument lies in the north wall, next to the door, and is reputed to be that of Good Sir James Douglas who died in Spain while on his way to the Holy Land with the heart of King Robert in 1331. The effigy, which was probably completed soon after his death, shows a knight drawing a sword, his head resting on a pillow and his feet on an animal; the canopy is of much later date, possibly 15th century. To the east of Good Sir James lies the monument of Archibald, 5th Earl of Douglas, who died in 1438. He is depicted wearing robes of state with a ducal coronet on his head, and his feet lie on a lion couchant. The surrounding monument (of mid 15th-century date) is more elaborate than that of Sir James, with a lower frieze bearing a number of carved figures which probably represent members of his family, and, above the ogee arch, a parapet pierced with quatrefoils.

A third monument lies on the opposite wall of the church; it contains the effigies of James, 7th Earl of Douglas and his wife Beatrice de Sinclair. The Earl died in 1443 and, from the inscription on the tomb, it is possible to establish that the monument was erected some time between 1448 and 1451. It is somewhat simpler than the two others described so far but this is probably a reflection of its later date. The Earl is shown in armour, his wife wears a flowing robe, and both have their hands clasped in prayer. Once again the lower frieze is decorated with a series of carved figures representing their six sons and four daughters. The inscriptions on the tombs of the two Earls style them both 'Duke of Touraine', a title granted to the 4th Earl in 1423 by Charles VII of France in recognition of his valiant efforts in the royal service. The remaining medieval monument is situated at the south-west end of the

choir; it is of early date and consists of a rather worn effigy of a woman with her feet resting on a bunch of foliage. In the centre of the church lies the Victorian marble tomb of the 7th Countess of Home, and at the west end there is a collection of architectural fragments including a number of Romanesque pieces which are the only traces of the earlier church.

St Bride's Church, Douglas: aerial view

St Bride's Church: the clock tower
(Above)

Tomb of Good Sir James Douglas
(Left)

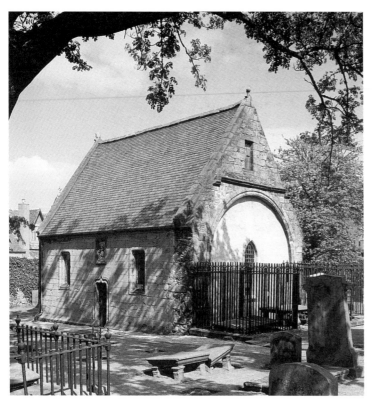

Skelmorlie Burial Aisle, Largs

64* Skelmorlie Burial Aisle, Largs, North Ayrshire

17th century.

NS 202594. The Skelmorlie aisle is situated in the burial-ground of the former parish church. To reach it, follow the signpost that points up a sidewalk which leads N off Largs Main Street, a little to the NW of the railway station.

Historic Scotland.

The Skelmorlie burial aisle is all that now survives of the former 'old kirk' of Largs and is renowned for its unusual burial monument and fine painted ceiling. Sir Robert Montgomery of Skelmorlie added the aisle to the church in 1636 to serve as a burial place for himself and his wife, Dame Margaret Douglas, and when the church was demolished in 1802 the aisle was left as a freestanding building.

The aisle is entered from the west through an unusual doorway above which there is a painted armorial panel bearing the arms of Montgomery and Eglinton (for Sir Robert) and those of Douglas

and Mar (for Dame Margaret). Inside there is an elaborate Renaissance-style burial monument which forms the focal point of the interior. It is without parallel in Scotland and is remarkable for the refinement of its Netherlandish detail. Carved from local freestone, it takes the form of a triumphal archway surmounted by strapwork, finials and cherubs, and is raised on a dais or gallery over a burial-vault which still contains the lead coffins of Sir Robert and his wife. Originally, the monument would have been brightly painted, like the armorial panel above the doorway, and was designed to include a pair of recumbent effigies but either these have not survived or they were never added. Today, an iron helm has been placed in the position that should have been occupied by the effigies. The design of the monument is probably based on Anglo-Dutch models and engravings, the construction itself being carried out by local craftsmen.

The ceiling of the aisle is a boarded barrel-vault richly embellished with painted decoration, in a style fashionable during the first half of the 17th century. It is, however, rare to see such decoration in a church as it is normally found only in secular contexts. The framework of the decoration is designed to imitate a stone vault, with painted scenes filling the spaces formed by the ribs. Included within the decoration there are texts from the Geneva Bible (popular in Scotland prior to the introduction of the King James version), signs of the zodiac and the imaginary arms of the tribes of Israel. Above the texts there are six scenes; those at the corners represent the four seasons, with Summer (behind and to the left of the monument) showing the aisle and the old kirk, while at the centre there are two prospects of Largs itself. An inscription gives the name of the painter as J Stalker and the date 1638.

The graveyard contains at least two other features of note. Firstly, the rectangular burial-vault of the Brisbane family which lies to the west of the custodian's office. Sir Thomas Brisbane was appointed governor-general of New South Wales, Australia in 1821, and gave his name to the state capital. Secondly, tucked in between the Brisbane vault and the graveyard wall, there is a reconstructed bronze-age cist, moved to its present position after discovery elsewhere in the parish.

EARLY CHRISTIAN MONUMENTS

Barochan Cross before it's removal to Paisley Abbey

Although west central Scotland contains a number of important settlement and ecclesiastical sites dating to the early historic period, the visible remains are largely limited to a range of carved stone monuments associated with the early Church. Documentary sources indicate that there were major settlements at Dumbarton Rock (no. 36) and Stirling (no. 38), but little or nothing remains to be seen at either site (for another possible late fort, see Dumyat, no. 87). The same is true at many of the ecclesiastical foundations, such as Govan (no. 66) and Glasgow Cathedral (no. 54), where the early sites have continued in use and are now covered by later buildings. Elsewhere, without the aid of excavation, it is impossible to distinguish those forts that continued to be used, or indeed were constructed, in the early historic period from those occupied during the earlier part of the iron age.

The early Church acted as a stimulus for the development of a vigorous tradition of stone carving which originated in the 5th and 6th centuries and continued until the Celtic Church was suppressed in the 12th century. None of the stones described here is as early as the 6th century, and the majority date to the later part of the period (10th-12th centuries) with a few examples from the 8th and 9th centuries. The carving, like the better known and closely related tradition of illuminated manuscripts, was carried out at ecclesiastical sites, and the stones are still found at church sites, even if in some cases (eg Barochan, no. 65; Hamilton, no. 67; Inchinnan, no. 68) the stones have been moved on more than one occasion.

The stones fall into two main series: commemorative crosses (Govan, no. 66, 3 and 4; Barochan, no. 65; Hamilton, no. 67), erected in honour of a saint, possibly the founder of the particular site, and burial-markers (Inchinnan, no. 68; Govan, no. 66, 2 and 5), which range from upright crosses to recumbent slabs and the Scandinavian inspired hogback tombstones (for other examples, see the hogback and two cross-slabs in the churchyard at Luss, Dumbarton, NS 361928). Also associated with burials are the two remarkable fragments of richly carved sarcophagi to be found at Govan and Inchinnan which belong to a small group of elaborately decorated tombs dating to the 10th-11th centuries.

The north-east boundary of west central Scotland overlaps that of southern Pictland but the main area of Pictish sculpture lies farther to the north and east and only one Pictish stone survives in Dunblane Cathedral (no. 53).

Govan
Sarcophagus

65 Barochan, Early Christian Cross, Paisley Abbey, Renfrewshire

8th century.

NS 485639. The cross is situated in the SW corner of the nave of Paisley Abbey (see no. 59).

Historic Scotland.

This cross has been moved from Barochan and, after much needed conservation, it has been re-erected in the shelter of Paisley Abbey. The stone has had a chequered history, having been moved on at least one previous occasion, and serves as a timely reminder of the portability of even comparatively large monuments. It was first recorded standing a little to the south of Mill of Barochan (NS 404698) from whence it was removed in the late 19th century to the top of a prominent knoll opposite Corsliehill (NS 405690).

It is an erect standing cross of pale, probably local, sandstone which rises to a height of 3.4 m, the lower 0.9 m of which would normally be buried. The decoration is badly weathered and the stone as a whole has deteriorated much in recent times, but viewed from a distance it is not difficult to imagine it in its former glory. Interlace forms the principal decorative motif with, on the front and rear faces, panels of human and animal sculpture. The front panel is divided into three zones: a mounted warrior carrying a spear confronting a man holding a drinking horn, at the top; a small human figure flanked by two men, one of whom holds an axe, at the centre; and, at the bottom, a pair of beasts facing one another (the latter are similar to a pair of animals on the side of the first stone described at Inchinnan, no. 68). On the rear there are two panels, with the bottom half of the upper and the top half of the lower bearing human figures. The upper four figures wear cloaks, and those in the lower panel carry spears and are blowing horns. The cross cannot be dated accurately but it is probably early in the Strathclyde series of sculptured stones and may be as early as the 8th century.

66 Old Parish Church, Govan, Early Christian Stones, Glasgow

10th to 12th centuries.

NS 553658. The Old Parish Church lies in the centre of Govan and is set back from the N side of Govan Road next to the Pearce Institute. The church is not always open but access may be arranged by contacting the minister.

Govan church contains one of the finest collections of Early Christian stones in Scotland. Originally, the stones lay in the graveyard but in 1926 they were moved into the church to preserve them from further decay. There are some forty-one stones in all and for the purposes of description they have been divided into a number of groups.

Govan, Old Parish Church: sarcophagus

Govan, Old Parish Church: hogback tombstone

1 Sarcophagus. The most unusual and interesting of the stones is the lower half of a sarcophagus which lies in the chancel. Its four sides are elaborately decorated with animals and interlace, the inspiration for which is derived from both Pictish and Anglian (Northumbrian) sources. The sarcophagus cannot be closely dated but it was probably carved in the 10th or 11th century.

2 Hogback Tombstones. Five hogbacks are present in Govan Church and this constitutes the largest single collection of this unusual type of grave-slab in Scotland. The stones are exceptionally large and take the form of a bow-sided, rectangular house with a distinctive curve to the roof-ridge (hence the term hogback). On the upper part of the stones the decoration consists of representations of wooden shingles (roof-tiles) and beasts (usually interpreted as bears). Although the ultimate origin for this tomb-type lies in Viking Scandinavia, they were probably introduced to Scotland and northern England via the Norse settlements in Ireland, and all five were carved in the 10th century.

3 Cross-shafts. The church contains fragments of two standing crosses, both of which have lost their cross-heads, and only parts of the cross-shafts now survive. The better preserved shaft, which stood for a while at Jordanhill, is 1.68 m high and copiously decorated. One of the faces bears a man on horseback, while elsewhere the decoration is principally of panels of different forms of interlace. The second cross is badly damaged and is decorated with interlace, but in one panel there is a scene representing St Paul and St Anthony breaking bread in the desert. These two stones are probably the earliest in Govan and date to about AD 900. Crosses of this type were usually commemorative and were dedicated to a local Celtic saint.

4 Upright Crosses. Unlike the two cross-shafts, the two upright crosses in the church marked the positions of individual interments, standing either at the head or foot of the grave. The more interesting of the two has a cross on its front face filled with interlaced grooved plaits flanked by intertwined serpents, and below there is a panel containing a horseman carrying a spear. On the back the principal feature is a boss with four serpents (a similar feature, but with two serpents, appears on the Hamilton Cross, no. 67). The upright crosses date to about the 10th century.

5 Recumbent Slabs. The largest group of stones at Govan comprise recumbent slabs or grave-markers which are placed around the walls of the church. The rectangular or oval slabs were laid over the grave and, in some cases, may have been accompanied by a headstone or cross. The decoration normally consists of a central cross and interlace; at Govan the quality of this decoration is rather indifferent but this is compensated for by the wide range of motifs employed. Grave-markers of this type are not closely datable and the Govan stones probably belong to the period AD 900–1200.

67 Hamilton, Early Christian Cross, South Lanarkshire

10th century.

NS 723555. This cross stands in the graveyard of Hamilton Parish Church which is situated to the S of Cadzow Street about 150 m SE of the municipal buildings.

This cross formerly stood in Hamilton Low Parks (NS 727567) close to the site of an early church, and was moved to its present position in 1926. Carved from a slab of local red sandstone, it stands to a height of 2.1 m and is decorated on all four sides.

The front bears (from top to bottom) a human figure between two beast-headed humans; a fish; a spiral boss between two panels of geometric carving in the arms of the cross; a panel of interlace in the shaft; and finally, a much weathered four-footed animal. On the rear, there is a squatting human figure above a central boss from which radiate two snake-like bands. The sides are also decorated: on the right, a beast-headed man and, below the cross-arm, an inverted human figure; on the left, a coiled snake, and, on the shaft, two beast-headed men and an animal with a long jaw.

Hamilton Cross, front face

The style of decoration suggests that the cross is rather late, probably dating to the 10th century.

68 Inchinnan, New Parish Church, Early Christian Stones, Renfrewshire

10th to 12th centuries.

NS 479689. From the A 8 take the side-road to Inchinnan village, the church is on the left after 350 m. The stones lie in a covered area between the church and the bell-tower.

The three decorated stones now preserved at the new parish church of Inchinnan were moved to their present position in 1965 when the site of the former medieval church was incorporated into Glasgow Airport. Inchinnan was probably an early Celtic foundation dedicated to St Conval, an Irish saint of the 5th or 6th century, and it served as the mother church for the area known later as Strathgryffe (the former county of Renfrew).

Hamilton Cross, rear face (Left)

Inchinnan sarcophagus, side view

decorated with friezes of beasts, while the head has a panel of interlace and on the base there is a coiled serpent. It is not possible to date the carving on this stone closely but it was probably produced about AD 900.

The earliest and most important of the three stones has been placed at the centre of the group. It is probably a shrine or sarcophagus cover, and is decorated on its sides as well as its upper face. In the centre of the upper face there is a cross with interlaced knobs at the base, with two pairs of opposed beasts above the cross, and a human figure and four beasts below. The lower scene represents Daniel in the lions' den, which was a popular motif in Early Christian art. The two long sides are

The red sandstone slab to the right of the sarcophagus cover is a fragment of an upright cross. Each of the three visible faces is divided into three panels of interlace with the central panel of each face filled with ornament. The cross probably dates to the 10th or 11th century, and was used as a grave-marker.

The final stone is a recumbent grave-slab bearing a long-shafted cross similar to several of the grave-slabs at Govan (no. 66) and dates from the 10th to 12th centuries.

Inchinnan graveslab

Inchinnan cross-shaft (Middle)

Inchinnan sarcophagus, top (Right)

ROMAN MONUMENTS

**Watling Lodge,
Antonine Wall**

The principal surviving Roman remains in west central Scotland are those of the Antonine Wall; all the major sections are described below and are arranged in order from east to west. Also included are two fortlets in Renfrewshire which form the westward continuation of the Wall, as well as a fortlet along the main Roman road into central Scotland through Clydesdale from the west end of Hadrian's Wall.

The Antonine Wall

The history of the Wall is outlined in the introduction and it is only necessary here to describe some of the details of the frontier system. The Roman army exercised control in potentially hostile areas by establishing a series of strong-points (forts, fortlets, etc) and linking them by roads which allowed troops to move quickly to deal with any trouble. This pattern can be seen along the supply route to Scotland up the line of the modern A 74 where there is a series of forts, about a day's march apart, accompanied by smaller posts, such as Redshaw Burn (no. 81). The frontier across the Forth-Clyde isthmus followed a similar pattern with a line of forts and smaller fortlets linked by a road (the Military Way) and, in this case, a physical barrier, the Wall itself. For the Roman troops, it was not a frontier in the sense of the Berlin Wall, as they were able to patrol well beyond its limits, but for the native population it marked a real divide, separating Roman from tribal Britain.

Some seventeen forts are known or suspected along the Wall (three are described in detail, nos 73, 75, 78); they are disposed at intervals of about three to five kms and range in area from 0.2 ha to 2.6 ha, with Rough Castle (no. 73) being one of the smallest. They were manned by up to 500 auxiliary troops for, although the Wall was built by the more highly trained legionaries, the job of patrolling the frontier was left to the less skilled forces. Filling the gaps between the larger forts, there are a number of smaller posts (fortlets), of which Kinneil (no. 69) is the most accessible, and these were manned by detachments drawn from the neighbouring forts. Also found at various points along the Wall, and usually occurring in groups, are the so-called 'expansions' (see nos 72, 73, 75) which are thought to be beacon-stances or signalling platforms of some sort. Their precise function or functions, are unknown, but it is likely that they served as some form of warning system, perhaps associated with troops operating to the north of the Wall.

Kinneil; reconstruction of the Roman fortlet and Antonine Wall

69 Antonine Wall, Fortlet, Kinneil, Falkirk

Mid 2nd century.

NS 977803. Follow the directions for Kinneil House (see no. 26), walk around the S side of the former walled garden and follow the track along the N side of Kinneil Wood. The fortlet lies on the crest of a slight rise 500 m WSW of Kinneil House. Alternatively, after visiting the House follow the signs for Kinneil Church and cross the fields from there to the fortlet.

In the Country Park at Kinneil House, a fortlet and a short stretch of the Antonine rampart have been partially reconstructed. The fortlet was only discovered in 1977 and has subsequently been excavated, showing that the interior measured 21 m from north to south by 18 m transversely within a bank 3 m thick. Like the Antonine Wall, the bank around the fortlet was built on a stone base, but, instead of being constructed entirely of turves, it had an earthen core revetted by turf.

There were two entrances, one on the north leading through the Antonine Wall, and a second on the south, connecting the fortlet to the Military Way (not visible). Within the interior, and now marked by short wooden uprights, there were the traces of post-holes, which formed two timber buildings used to house the garrison, as well as the remains of stout gateways at the two entrances. Outside the

fortlet further protection was provided by a shallow ditch which abutted the Wall on the east and west.

Besides the better known and much larger forts attached to the rear of the Antonine Wall, there is also a series of smaller fortlets, to which Kinneil belongs. Some nine have been discovered so far but it is likely that they were originally placed at intervals of about 1.6 km along the entire length of the Wall. Their precise function is not known but, on plan at least, they appear to be equivalent to the milecastles along Hadrian's Wall.

70 Antonine Wall, Callendar House, Falkirk

Mid 2nd century.

NS 896796. About 1 km E of the centre of Falkirk take a side-turning S from the A 9 following a signpost for the Callendar Park Leisure Centre. Leave the car in the first parking area.

Some 400 m of the Wall is preserved in the former policies of Callendar House, where it makes use of a slight ridge that runs almost parallel to the main road. The Wall itself has been reduced to little more than a low mound and the most obvious feature is the ditch which is flanked on the north by the remains of the so-called 'upcast mound'. As the name suggests this mound is composed of material

**Callendar House,
Antonine Wall**

dug out of the ditch during its construction; the upcast was not required for the Wall and was normally deposited as a low mound immediately to the north of the ditch. Because of its stony composition, it frequently survives better than the turf of the Wall, and there is little wonder that at least one 18th-century antiquary was misled, for a while, into believing that the Wall lay to the north of the ditch, not to the south.

71 Antonine Wall, Watling Lodge, Falkirk

Mid 2nd century.

NS 863798. Take the road (B 816) from Camelon to High Bonnybridge (Tamfourhill Road) and follow the signposts. The Wall flanks the S side of the road for about 300 m E of the house called Watling Lodge.

Historic Scotland/NTS.

Set on the edge of a steep north-facing scarp, this section of the Wall contains the most impressive stretch of the ditch to survive. Here it retains the original V-shaped cross-section, measuring 12 m across by up to 4.5 m in depth, and gives a stark reminder of the difficulties of crossing this barrier, particularly when one considers that the Wall rose at least a further 3 m behind the lip of the ditch. Little can now be seen of the Wall itself, but excavation has revealed the presence of the stone plinth on which the turves were stacked (see no. 77). This section of the Wall was of special

**Rough Castle:
prehistoric field
system**

importance as it flanked the point when the main Roman road from the south crossed the Wall on its way up to the fort at Ardoch (Braco), Perthshire and on into Strathearn. The actual site of the gateway, and the fort that guarded it, is now under Watling Lodge and no trace of it can be seen.

72 Antonine Wall, Tentfield, Falkirk

Mid 2nd century.

NS 856798. Take the Camelon to High Bonnybridge road (B 816) and park immediately W of the crossing with Lime Road.

The finest surviving stretches of the Wall lie between Bonnyside House (NS 834798) and Watling Lodge (see no. 71), a distance of some 3 km, and within this sector examples of most of the principal features of the Wall can be seen, as well as the major fort at Rough Castle (no. 73).

To the west of Lime Road the Wall itself is particularly well preserved and it still stands to a height of over 1 m. Some 160 m west of Lime Road there is a beacon stance attached to the rear of the rampart (visible as a prominent mound projecting from the wall); another lies further to the west, a short distance east of the abandoned railway line, but it is more difficult to make out as it is partially obscured by trees in Tentfield Plantation. When the vegetation is low the line of the Military Way can be seen as a slight mound beginning a little to the north-east of the point where the road (B 816) crosses the railway; it can be traced for a short distance before being lost in Tentfield Plantation.

73 Antonine Wall, Fort, Rough Castle, Falkirk

Mid 2nd century.

NS 843798. The fort is signposted from High Bonnybridge and Bonnyside; access is along the tarmacked road to Bonnyside Farm, then via a rough track to a carpark at NS 841798. If approaching from Bonnybridge, look out for a colourful mural on the gable end of the foundry by the bridge over the canal (NS 824800).

Historic Scotland/NTS.

Rough Castle, Roman fort and Antonine Wall: aerial view

The best-preserved section of the Antonine Wall lies between Bonnyside House (NS 834799) and the fort at Rough Castle. This section includes fine stretches of the rampart and ditch, with the remains of two signalling platforms, traces of the Military Way and the most complete of the Wall forts.

The fort and its annexe lie at the east end of this section of the Wall and occupy a carefully chosen position in the angle between the rampart and the gully of the Rowantree Burn. Rough Castle is one of the smallest of the forts along the Wall (0.4 ha) and it was excavated in 1904 (the remains of the stone buildings found at the time have been reburied). The fort was defended by a turf rampart that was butted on to the Wall sometime after the latter's construction, but they were both part of the same plan, as a causeway had been left by the ditch diggers to allow access to the fort from the north. The Military Way entered the fort through the West Gate, after crossing the Rowantree Burn on a wooden bridge, whence it became the principal road in the fort before leaving again by the East Gate; a by-pass for through-traffic along the Military Way ran around the south side of the defences.

An annexe was built on to the more open east flank of the fort; it was defended by a rampart and single ditch on the south, but on the east there were two additional, rather widely spaced, ditches. The annexes to Wall forts provided extra space but also served as ideal locations for bath-houses which were considerable fire-risks if placed within the forts themselves. The excavators reburied the bath-house but the remains of a comparable building, also located in a fort annexe, can be seen at Bearsden fort, no. 78. An unusual feature of the defences at Rough Castle, and only discovered because of the excavation, is a regular series of pits, which concealed sharpened stakes, lying to the north-west of the causeway across the Wall ditch. These pits, known as lillia (lillies), were designed to break up any massed attack on the vulnerable gateway through the Wall.

Rough Castle: Antonine Wall during excavation, showing clearly defined turves resting on the stone base

**Rough Castle,
Roman fort and
Antonine Wall:
plan**

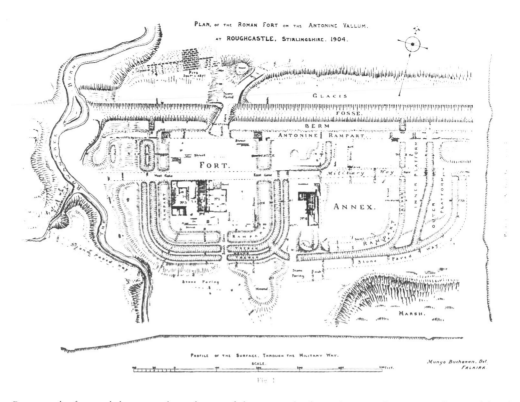

**Rough Castle,
Roman fort and
Antonine Wall:
lillia during
excavation in
1904**

Between the fort and the car park, and west of the car park, the Wall and ditch survive in good condition. About 60 m west of the cattle-grid at the entrance to the site, there is a beacon- or signalling-stance attached to the rear of the Wall, and another is situated closer to Bonnyside House. In this section the Military Way lies beneath the modern track, but its course is marked by a series of quarry-pits visible between the rear of the Wall and the

track; these pits were dug to provide gravel for the Roman causeway.

Lying on the slope between the fort and the railway line (NS 845797), there are the remains of a field-system composed of embanked fields. The precise date of the system is not known, but it probably belongs to the prehistoric period.

Finds from the fort are preserved in the National Museums of Scotland, Edinburgh.

74 Antonine Wall, Seabegs Wood, Falkirk

Mid 2nd century.

NS 814793. Seabegs Wood lies on the S side of the Castlecary to Bonnybridge Road about 1.5 km W of Bonnybridge; signposted.

Historic Scotland/NTS.

Preserved in the vestiges of Seabegs Wood there is a good stretch of the Wall which includes the best-surviving section of the Military Way. The Wall was built just above a marked break in slope giving it the maximum military advantage and offering a clear view over the valley of the Bonny Water. The

Seabegs Wood,
Antonine Wall:
the ditch

ditch is about 12 m broad but for much of its length it is waterlogged and choked with vegetation. To the north, the upcast mound is clearly visible, and on the south the narrow berm between the inner lip of the ditch and the base of the Wall appears as a distinct terrace. The Wall itself is comparatively well-preserved and still stands to a maximum height of 1.2 m. The most interesting feature of this section of the Wall, however, is the Military Way which runs obliquely at the rear of the rampart and is separated from it by about 40 m at the east end.

It appears as a cambered mound, 7 m wide and no more than 0.3 m in height, and can be distinguished as a parch-mark in dry periods. Traces of its metalling and larger stone-bottoming can be seen exposed in the sides of recent drainage channels which have been cut through it.

75 Antonine Wall, Croy Hill, North Lanarkshire

Mid 2nd century.

NS 725762–743770. Take the Kilsyth to Cumbernauld road (B 802) and follow signposts from the W end of Croy Village.

Historic Scotland.

Between the village of Croy and Dullatur there is a well-preserved section of the ditch, which may be approached from the east end, if preferred; the most noteworthy length, however, lies between Croy Village and the fort on Croy Hill. The only section of the rampart to survive in this area is situated north-east of Croy Village, on the west flank of Croy Hill; it was partially excavated in the late 19th century and was shown to stand to a height of 1.5 m with a battered or sloping front

Seabegs Wood,
Antonine Wall:
aerial view
showing the ditch
running through
the wood
adjacent to the
Forth and Clyde
Canal (Left)

Croy Hill, Antonine Wall: part of Roman tombstone showing three legionaries, possibly a father and two sons, found close to the fort

Croy Hill, Antonine Wall: the ditch making it's way across the hill with a large 'crows foot' spoil-tip in the foreground

face. Also preserved in this short section of rampart are two beacon- or signalling-platforms built against the back of the Wall, which appear as low mounds at either end of the surviving rampart.

The fort lies 600 m to the north-east, on the east flanks of the hill; little can now be seen but excavations earlier this century revealed parts of the headquarters building, and a number of inscribed stones from the Croy Hill area show that

a detachment of the Sixth Legion worked here at one period. The fort (now marked by a clump of trees) was attached to the rear of the Wall; a gap was left in the Wall for the fort gateway but no corresponding causeway was left in the ditch which was presumably crossed by a wooden bridge. More recent excavations have revealed the presence of an earlier fortlet (backing on to the Wall to the west of the fort) and traces of a possible civilian settlement (a vicus) to the south-west accompanied by a field-system on the south-east.

The steepness of the north face of Croy Hill and the hardness of the rock posed considerable problems for the Wall builders. Much of the ditch in this sector is cut into extremely hard volcanic rock, and immediately north-north-east of the fort they finally gave up, leaving a portion of the ditch unexcavated. To the west of the fort the ground falls steeply to the north, and instead of dispensing with the ditch altogether and relying on the natural defences, the line of the ditch was swung westwards and doggedly continued below the steep face of the hill.

76 Antonine Wall, Bar Hill, East Dunbartonshire

Mid 2nd century.

NS 707759. Follow the signposts from Twechar and walk to the wood on the top of the hill.

Historic Scotland.

The fort on Bar Hill, which has recently been laid out for public display by Historic Scotland, lies on the highest stretch (150 m) of the Antonine Wall, and commands fine views of the Campsie Fells to the north, as well as along the Wall to the west, and, during the Roman period, would also have overlooked a long stretch of the Wall to the east.

Bar Hill was one of the earliest forts to have been recognised by antiquarians; excavations were first carried out in 1902–05, and further work was undertaken in 1978–82 before the fort was opened to the public. Unlike Rough Castle (no. 73), the fort on Bar Hill is not attached to the Antonine Wall but stands about 30 m to the south. Ploughing has reduced the turf rampart and the ditches to gentle surface undulations, and the only immediately

Bar Hill Roman Fort: excavations in progress

recognisable section of the defences lie on the east, where the causeway of a road can be seen crossing the double ditches and entering the gateway to the fort. The defences enclose an area covering about 1.3 ha and the recent excavations have exposed the remains of some of the stone-walled buildings within the interior. These include the centrally-placed headquarters building with a well in its courtyard, a granary, and the bath-house. The latter is an unusual feature to find within the ramparts of a fort, as, for reasons of fire safety, they were normally placed well away from the barrack-blocks and other timber buildings (compare this with the siting of the bath-house at Bearsden, no. 78).

Inscriptions from within, or close to, the fort have identified two of the units garrisoned there–the First Cohort of Hamians and the First Cohort of Baetasians. The Hamian archers, who were originally from Syria, were a specialised unit of archers and parts of their bows were recovered during the excavations. The Baetasian cohort was raised on the lower Rhine and after leaving Bar Hill served at the western end of Hadrian's Wall.
The finds from the excavations are preserved in the Hunterian Museum, University of Glasgow.

77 Antonine Wall, New Kilpatrick Cemetery, East Dunbartonshire

Mid 2nd century.

NS 556724. New Kilpatrick Cemetery lies on the N side of Boclair Road (B 8099) 700 m E of its junction with the A 81 Park on Boclair Road.

There are two stretches of the stone base of the Wall exposed in the cemetery at New Kilpatrick. Excavated in 1902 and 1922 respectively, they were subsequently consolidated and now offer the best opportunity to view the basal plinth of the Wall. To reach the first section enter the cemetery and continue along the main pathway until the toilets have been passed on the right; the path then divides, take the middle course follow on until it curves to the right, the Wall is then in the grass to the right exposed in the bottom of a trench.

The stone base measures about 4.5 m in breadth with an inner and outer boulder kerb retaining a rubble core, which is little more than one course deep. An interesting feature visible in this section is the step method of construction. This has been recorded in many places along the Wall and was

New Kilpatrick Cemetery: Drainage channel through the stone base of the Antonine Wall (Top)

Excavated stone base of the Antonine Wall (Right)

evidently used on steep slopes, such as this, to provide a more level base for the turf superstructure in order to prevent it from slumping downslope. Also visible in this section is a water culvert which passes through the base of the Wall. These were necessary to allow for the passage of surface water which was otherwise interrupted by the Wall; without them water would have ponded up behind the Wall and eventually led to its collapse.

The second section lies towards the east wall of the cemetery–to reach it, continue up the slope towards the Mausoleum and turn slightly to the right. This portion is similar to the first, except that as it is not built on a slope it is not stepped, and it thus more typical of the Wall as a whole. Although situated on the crest of a knoll, this stretch is also cut by a

drainage culvert, suggesting that they must have been built at regulation intervals regardless of whether they were actually required.

78 Bearsden Bath-house, East Dunbartonshire

Mid 2nd century.

NS 546720. The bath-house lies at 35 Roman Road, on the N side of the street about 350 m E of its junction with the A 809. Visitors arriving by car should leave their vehicle in the public carpark 250 m W of the bath-house.

Historic Scotland.

The Antonine Wall fort at Bearsden (also known as New Kilpatrick) was largely obliterated by housing in the last century and was thought to be lost to archaeology, but redevelopment of part of the site in the 1970s gave the opportunity to investigate the remains. The Victorian builders had done far less damage to the fort than had been expected, largely because the site was on a slope and much levelling up had been undertaken, thus preserving the Roman remains. Consequently, it was possible to recover much of the plan of the buildings within the fort. The most spectacular find, however, lay in the annexe attached to the east rampart. Here, the excavators uncovered the remains of a bath-house which has proved to be one of the best surviving examples in Scotland. Bath-houses were essential installations at Roman forts, filling a vital role in the social life of the troops rather than simply serving as an ablutions block. They were normally sited outside the fort, well away from the timber buildings, because of the risk of fire from the furnaces. Although the area of the bath-house was scheduled for building, the developers (Woodblane Developments Ltd) generously agreed to its preservation.

The bath-house is a long rectangular building with three projecting wings, one on the north and two on the south. The west half, which was used for changing and relaxing in, was built of timber, stone only being used where essential in the heated section of the baths on the east. (The position of the timber wall-posts are now indicated by short wooden uprights.) The bathing suite consisted of three elements: a hot, dry room, which projects

Bearsden Roman fort: the excavated bath-house

Stone head of the goddess Fortuna (Top Left)

from the north wall of the main building; a hot steam range, comprising the three rooms (increasing in temperature from west to east) leading directly off the entrance hall with a hot plunge bath opening off the hottest room; a cold plunge bath, which projects from the south wall opposite the hot/dry room. Thus the bather had the choice of a hot/dry bath followed by a cold plunge or he could move progressively through the hot/steam range to a dip in the hot plunge bath before returning to finish with a cold plunge. The bath-house was so well-preserved that it retained many interesting constructional details including hypocaust floors and walls, stoke-holes, wall plaster and even the remains of stone benches. Finds from this site are on display in the Hunterian Museum, University of Glasgow.

79 Lurg Moor, Fortlet, Inverclyde

Mid 2nd century.

NS 295737. From Greenock take the Kilmalcolm Road (B 788) and follow it until open country is reached, then park before passing a mast on the N. Walk up the bank of the westernmost of the three streams which crosses the road by the mast, and turn W at the third fence-line. The fortlet lies 230 m W of the point where the stream is crossed by the fence.

Like the west flank of Hadrian's Wall, along the Cumbrian coast, the western flank of the Antonine frontier was protected by a series of stations along the south Clyde coast. The first was a fort at Bishopton, situated on the south bank of the Clyde opposite the end of the Wall at Old Kilpatrick; the second, and best preserved of the series, is this fortlet on Lurg Moor (for the third see Outerwards, no. 80). Rectangular on plan, the fortlet measures 43 m by 49 m over a turf rampart accompanied by an outer ditch; on the east and west where the defences are particularly well-preserved, the bottom of the ditch is up to 2 m below the crest of the rampart. The single entrance lies on the south and, leading out of it for a distance of 100 m, there is a causeway 4.5 m wide, which probably represents the remains of the road leading towards the next fortlet at Outerwards (no. 80).

Although no excavation has been carried out on this site, several sherds of Antonine pottery have been found immediately outside the fortlet, and there is little doubt that it dates to the Antonine period. The internal arrangements were probably similar to those at Outerwards with a pair of wooden buildings providing accommodation for a small permanent garrison.

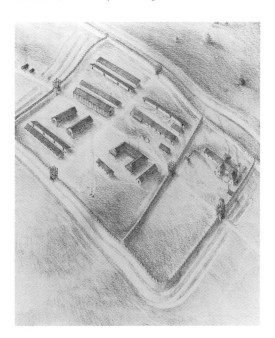

Bearsden Roman fort: reconstruction drawing of the fort (Left)

80 Outerwards, Fortlet, North Ayrshire

Mid 2nd century.

NS 232666. Take the minor road from Largs to Outerwards farmsteading (NS 234661). Follow the field boundary that runs NW from the farm, cross the stream and continue along the edge of the field until the crest of the ridge is reached, then cross into the rough ground and continue NNE along the crest of the ridge for 300 m until the fortlet is reached.

The fortlet at Outerwards forms part of the westward continuation of the Antonine frontier system that guarded the Clyde approaches to the Wall (see also Lurg Moor, no. 79). It comprises a subsquare enclosure measuring 14.3 m across within a low (0.3 m) turf rampart, with two entrances. Further protection was provided by an irregular outer ditch which was interrupted by a causeway on the south-south-west, but there was no gap on the north-north-east corresponding to the entrance through the rampart. Excavation in 1970 showed that the fortlet contained two timber buildings and that it was occupied on two separate occasions within the Antonine period. Although the fortlet is only the size of a large watch-post (0.2 ha), the excavation showed that it had a permanent garrison and no internal tower. The site, however, commands extensive views over the Firth of Clyde and would have functioned in much the same way as the fortlets along the line of the Antonine Wall, being linked by road to the fortlets further north and south in the chain.

81 Redshaw Burn, Fortlet, South Lanarkshire

Mid 2nd century.

NT 030139. Take the track to Nether Howcleuch farmsteading. Park and walk up the track that follows the W bank of the Redshaw Burn; from the point where the track enters the forestry plantation, strike eastwards and the fortlet lies immediately E of the Redshaw Burn.

This fortlet is one of a series of stations situated along the course of the main Roman road leading from the W end of Hadrian's Wall to west central Scotland. Unlike the present motorway, which

follows the floor of the Evan and Clyde Valleys, the Roman road avoided the low-lying ground, preferring a higher course to the east.

The fortlet is situated to the south of the Roman road, which runs along the forest boundary at this point. It is rectangular with rounded angles and measures 19.8 m by 17.4 m within a rampart 5.5 m thick and 0.3 m in height. There is a single entrance, 4 m wide, at the centre of the north side, from which a metalled trackway leads to the main Roman road. The more vulnerable east and south sides of the fortlet are protected by twin ditches, while on the west, where the Redshaw Burn forms a natural defence, only a single ditch was dug. At a date after the initial construction of the fortlet, an additional length of rampart and ditch was built running from the cliff above the Redshaw Burn and across the line of the earlier trackway. This provided an enclosure which probably served as a wagon park for vehicles moving up and down the road.

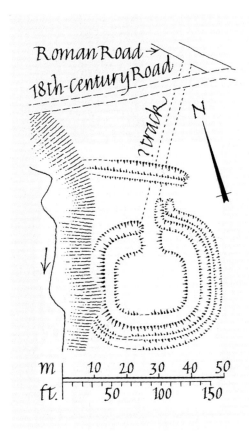

Redshaw Burn, Roman fortlet: plan (Right)

PREHISTORIC SETTLEMENT

Arbory Hill, fort

With the exception of the hut-circles on Machrie Moor (no. 95), most of the settlements described in this section date from about 1200 BC to the first centuries AD, and therefore span the periods sometimes referred to as the late bronze and iron ages. The long chronological span and the wide geographical spread of the area results in a broad range of settlement types being present, both of the open, undefended forms and of the enclosed or defended types. The best surviving remains are to be found in Clydesdale, where the open sheepwalks of the Southern Uplands have helped to preserve them against the ravages of agriculture and forestry.

The open settlements of Clydesdale, known as unenclosed platform settlements, form a compact group around the headwaters of the Clyde and Tweed, and create a distinctive settlement pattern of great interest. The examples chosen (nos 92-93) are in some ways exceptional in that they are sited close to other, possibly contemporary, monuments—a field-system at Ellershie Hill (no. 92) and a group of small cairns at Normangill Rig (no. 93)—for elsewhere they are normally isolated from other field monuments.

The enclosed settlements include a variety of forms ranging from strongly defended, multivallate forts (nos 82-83, 85-88), through less well protected settlements (nos 84, 90), to homesteads (no. 90) surrounded by comparatively slight banks and palisades. Many of the sites are multiperiod, and several appear to have undergone radical changes in their form over the centuries of occupation (nos 81-83, 86).

Inside some of the defended settlements there are still traces of the round timber houses to be seen as surface features (nos 84-86, 90), and from a study of the remains it is possible to show that several distinctive types of house were in use during the iron age. The principal forms found in Clydesdale are the ring-ditch and ring-groove houses, and both are variations on the post-ring round house which is found throughout Britain in the first millennium BC.

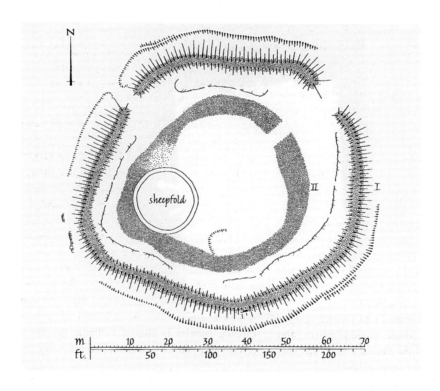

**Blackhill,
Crawfordjohn,
fort**

82 Arbory Hill, Fort, South Lanarkshire

Late 1st millennium BC.

NS 944238. From Abington Village cross the Clyde and take the minor road that flanks the E side of the valley. Follow it as far as the Raggengill Burn, park and climb to the top of Arbory Hill.

The elevated (429 m OD) and isolated position of this fort has led not only to the excellent preservation of its two-period defences but also to the rare survival (for Lanarkshire) of parts of its contemporary field-system. These features, combined with the magnificent view of Clydesdale gained from the summit, more than compensate for the arduous climb up from the road.

The earlier defences consist of two sets of ramparts with outer ditches and counterscarp banks. For the greater part of their circuit the ramparts are concentric and closely spaced but, on the east, their lines diverge creating a space that could have been used as a corral for cattle (such an interpretation is reinforced by the appearance of a staggered entrance at the mouth of the corral which would have aided the passage of stock). An unusual feature of this phase of the fort is the provision of five entrances; this seems excessive and would have weakened the defensive capacity of the fort.

In the second period, and in keeping with many other forts in Lanarkshire, the area to be defended, or at least enclosed, was reduced by about 50%. This time, instead of constructing ramparts and ditches, a stone walled enclosure was built and the number of entrances was reduced to two. Within the enclosure these are traces of three ring-ditch houses as well as a single house-platform, and between the wall and the Period 1 inner rampart there are several other vague platforms that may mark the sites of timber houses.

About 75 m east of the fort, there is a linear earthwork drawn across the neck of the saddle which leads to the higher ground beyond. Such earthworks are frequently found associated with forts in the Borders and were once thought to form some sort of outer defence line. Recent work, however, suggests that they are part of contemporary field-systems and acted as stock

barriers, keeping cattle away from the vicinity of the fort. This was necessary as the area immediately around the fort appears to have been cultivated, and air photographs taken when there was a light dusting of snow have revealed traces of narrow (c 1.2 m) cultivation ridges which radiate down the hill away from the outer rampart. Because these remains are so slight they can barely be seen from the ground; their discovery, however, has been one of the most significant recent developments in iron-age settlement studies, and examples of this cord rig have been found widely in the Border counties but, so far Arbory is the only known example in Lanarkshire.

83 Blackhill, Crawfordjohn, Fort, South Lanarkshire

Later 1st millennium BC.

NS 908239. Turn off the A 74 about 2 km NW of Abington and follow the minor road (signposted Crawfordjohn) as far as Duneaton Bridge.

Situated on an elevated spur but overlooked by higher ground, the position of this small fort is similar to that of Arbory Hill (no. 82). Like many of the other forts close by, the defences at Blackhill are of more than one period. In the first phase, it was surrounded by a single earth-and-stone rampart accompanied by an outer ditch which may never have been completed on the west, where there is an outcrop of rock. There are two entrances, and around the inner face of the rampart a quarry-scoop is visible. In the second period, an inner stone-walled enclosure was built, with a single entrance on the north-east, and the earlier rampart was strengthened by the addition of a stone capping (similar to that at Fallburn, no. 88). A recent sheepfold has been built in the interior.

About 200 m north-west of the fort, there is a linear earthwork similar to that at Arbory Hill (no. 82) and, as there, it is likely that this served to separate a cultivated area around the fort from the pasture beyond. Some 25 m outside the linear earthwork there is a small barrow, 6.5 m in maximum diameter and only 0.2 m high, surrounded by a shallow ditch 2 m wide; another burial-site, in this case a cairn lies 25 m west of the barrow (measuring 5.8 m in diameter, by 0.8 m in height), also surrounded by a ditch. Although such burials are normally ascribed to the bronze age, it is possible that they may be of considerably later date, contemporary with one phase of occupation of the fort.

84 Black Hill, Lesmahagow, Fort, Settlement and Cairn, South Lanarkshire

Later 1st millennium BC.

NS 832435. Black Hill is most readily approached via a minor road which crosses the S shoulder of the hill. Park to the W of a large gravel pit and walk up a track (NS 833431) which leads to the summit.

NTS.

This group of monuments lies on the rounded top of Black Hill (290 m OD) from which there are panoramic views over the Clyde Valley. The earliest

feature on the hill is a large bronze-age round cairn situated on the highest point; it has been reduced to a grass-grown mound, 18 m in diameter by 0.9 m in height, with several kerbstones visible on the west. Surmounting the cairn there is an Ordnance Survey triangulation pillar which is used as a control point in the preparation of OS maps. These pillars are normally situated in prominent positions and so are frequently found associated with hilltop archaeological sites.

Many of the forts described in this book are multi-period with the ramparts of the various phases piled up on one another; in this case, however, the earliest fort has been built to enclose the entire summit of the hill, while the later settlement has been tacked on to the south side of the fort, so the interiors of the two sites do not overlap. The oval fort is comparatively large, measuring 155 m by 108 m (1.67 ha) within a single stone wall which is now

Black Hill, Lesmahagow: aerial view

so ruined that it is no longer possible to detect any original entrances. Abutting the south side of the fort there is a settlement, defended for the most part by double banks with a medial ditch but, on the north, the wall of the fort has been incorporated into the circuit. There are at least two round-house sites in the interior, lying on the west immediately north of the entrance, and what may be others just to the south of the fort wall.

Without excavation it is impossible to tell how long a gap (if any) existed between the occupation of the fort and that of the settlement, but it is possible that the fort belongs to the earlier part of the iron age, while the settlement is likely to date to its later phases. The reason for the shift away from the summit, however, is not hard to guess, and must be related to the exposed nature of the hilltop and a desire to live on a slightly more sheltered section of the hill.

85 Camps Knowe Wood, Fort, South Lanarkshire

Late 1st millennium BC.

NT 013228. From Crawford take the minor road up the Camps Water Glen and follow the S side of Camps Reservoir (take care of the gates across the road in the Reservoir section) and park in a quarry which lies beside the stream between Kneesend Wood and Camps Knowe Wood.

This fort occupies the summit of a promontory-like knoll in the recently felled Camps Knowe Wood. The north and north-east flanks of the knoll fall steeply in Casan Cleuch, but on the south and south-west the slopes are more gradual and, in consequence, the defences have been developed in greater depth on these sides.

The defences consist of a series of earth-and-stone ramparts accompanied by ditches and their lay-out suggests that they were constructed in two, if not three, stages. In the earliest phase the summit area (measuring 70 m by 45 m) was protected by twin ramparts and medial ditch on the south and south-west (I and IA on the plan) and by a single rampart on the north and north-east. At that stage its defences closely resembled those at Fallburn (no. 88), Arbory (no. 82) and Period 2 at Cow Castle

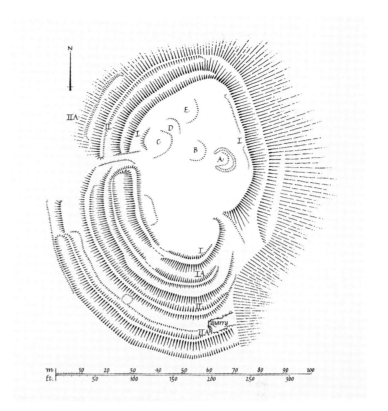

(no. 86). Subsequently the defences were strengthened, particularly on the more vulnerable southerly flanks, by the addition of an extra rampart (II) which was built from material thrown up from an inner ditch. On the north-east this line of defence is now visible only as a slight scarp and it is likely that in this sector the rampart was replaced by a simple timber palisade. The outermost rampart (IIA) may have been constructed at the same time as II, but because it is of a slightly different character and separated from II by a broad berm, it probably belongs to a slightly later period. On the south IIA consists of a rampart with an outer defensive ditch and the remains of a counterscarp bank and an internal quarry-scoop. For some reason this rampart and ditch was not continued as far as the west entrance and, to the north of it, is only represented by a slight bank. The fort was approached by two entrances, set at either end of the strongest section of the defences, with the western example probably serving as the principal access point. In the interior there are slight traces of at least four or five timber round-houses, but these are difficult to see under the vegetation that covers the site.

Camps Knowe Wood, fort

86 Cow Castle, Fort, South Lanarkshire

Later 1st millennium BC.

NT 042331. From Coulter take the side-road signposted to Culterallers and turn left on to the track to Nisbet Farm (NT 037328), then walk along the track that leads E from the farmyard to the knoll on which the fort is situated.

The gorge of the Culter Water provides access to an attractive group of minor valleys containing a remarkable collection of prehistoric and later monuments, which include at least six defended settlements, a crannog and numerous cultivation terraces.

The best preserved of the remains is the multi-period fort known as Cow Castle. On the ground its jumble of ramparts is difficult to disentangle, but with the aid of an aerial photograph and an interpretative plan, the various phases can be readily distinguished. Two main periods are represented, with the defences of the earlier work being partially overlain or reused in the later phase. In Period 1 the defences comprise two ramparts and ditches (1A and B) with, on the inner side of the south section of 1A, a quarry scoop dug to provide additional material for the rampart. Access was provided by two inturned gateways placed close to the steep north-west flank of the hill. This is a characteristic position for gateways on prehistoric earthworks, as it makes maximum use of the defensive potential of the site, while on similar medieval sites the entrances are frequently more centrally placed. In the second period the area enclosed was reduced in size with the construction of ramparts IIA and B, but wherever possible sections of the earlier defences were used. Traces of at least three ring-ditch houses are visible within the fort; one, on the north-east, appears to belong to Period 1 as its outer wall-line is cut by the Period II ditch, and the others were probably built during Period II (although their wall-lines must have become very close to the rampart).

Cow Castle, fort: aerial view

Plan (Bottom Right)

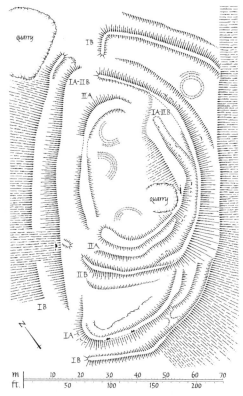

m   10   20   30   40   50   60   70
ft.   50   100   150   200

Dumyat, fort

87 Dumyat, Fort, Stirling

Late 1st millennium BC to early 1st millennium

NS 832973. The easiest way to approach Dumyat is to take the Sheriffmuir road from Bridge of Allan, park at NS 813980, then follow the footpath SE to the fort.

This multi-period fort occupies the south-west shoulder of Dumyat Hill and commands magnificent views over the Forth to Stirling and beyond. The interest of the fort lies not only in the remains of its impressive defences but also in considering the significance of its elevated position and in the derivation of its name.

The east side of the fort is protected by steep crags and the main weight of the defences are concentrated on the west. The earlier period is represented by two closely-set stone ramparts, enclosing an area which measures 130 m by 48 m, with an entrance on the west; outside the entrance there are a series of outworks abutting the ramparts. The later work lies around the highest point of the hill and is linked to the earlier rampart by a much ruined wall; it comprises a dun-like enclosure measuring 27 m by 16 m within a massive stone wall. Although the site is normally considered to be a multi-period fortification, with the dun-like enclosure built inside the remains of an earlier iron-age fort, it is possible that it may all be of one period. Recent excavations elsewhere, however, have shown that the sequence on sites such as this may be far more complex than the fieldwork evidence alone might suggest.

The location of the fort, standing at a height of over 300 m OD, raises questions about the nature of its occupation, economy and status. Its position is extremely exposed, well above the normal level of cultivation, and must have been a most unpleasant place to have spent the winter. Most forts are found at considerably lower altitudes, where all-year occupation is easier to comprehend, and we must consider whether the fort was ever intended for permanent settlement or was, perhaps, only used on a temporary basis for particular, short-term functions.

Although the summit to the north-east is now called Dumyat, it is possible that the name originally referred to the fort itself. Professor Watson considered that it might be interpreted as 'Dun Myat' (the Dun (fort) of the Maeatae). The Maeatae were a local late iron age/ Dark Age tribe and it is possible that they lent their name to the tribal capital. For another possible example of the association of a tribal name and an archaeological feature see the Clackmannan Stone (no. 95).

Fallburn, fort

88 Fallburn, Fort, South Lanarkshire

Late 1st millennium BC.

NS 961367. Access to this fort is from the same footpath that leads to the cairn on Tinto Hill (no. 102). Park at NS 964394 and follow the footpath for 700 m.

This well-preserved circular fort is situated on a slight knoll which offers little natural strength. The defences comprise twin ramparts and ditches with a slight counterscarp bank around the lip of much of the outer ditch. On top of the inner bank there are the remains of a stone wall which probably represents a second period of construction, thus resembling the sequence at Arbory Hill (no. 82) and Blackhill, Crawfordjohn (no. 83). The fort has two entrances but there are no traces of any houses in the interior and all that can be seen are a recent turf dyke and a slight scoop behind the rampart which was probably dug to provide extra material for the defences.

An almost carbon copy of this fort is to be found about 3 km to the north-north-west on the summit of Chester Hill (NS 953395), but it is not as well-preserved as Fallburn and does not have evidence for a second period

89 Walls Hill, Fort, Renfrewshire

Late 1st millennium BC.

NS 411588. This fort is most readily approached from North Castlewalls farmsteading—to reach the farm take the minor road that runs NE from Howwood and follow the farm road through Skiff Wood. Park and ask permission at North Castlewalls, then follow a trackway to the fort.

This exceptionally large fort occupies the summit (230 m OD) of a steep-sided lava plateau which, except on the north-west where it is overlooked by higher ground, dominates the surrounding farmland and forms a prominent local landmark. Roughly oval on plan, the fort measures 460 m by 200 m within the much denuded remains of a single stone-faced rampart which has been drawn around the lip of the plateau. The southern third of the interior has been cultivated and the defences largely removed, but on the north considerable stretches of the rampart remain, measuring up to 3.5 m in thickness by about 1 m in height. Only one original entrance passage is now visible and this lies on the north-north-east a short distance to the east of the point where the track from the farm breaks the rampart. No houses can be seen in the interior but excavations in 1956 revealed fragments of late iron-age pottery and pieces of worked jet or shale.

Walls Hill has attracted much attention as one of the largest prehistoric enclosures in Scotland, at about 7.5 ha being exceeded in area by only three other forts. Some writers have likened it to a Celtic oppidum (a large defended late iron-age town found in southern England and on the Continent) and have suggested that it is the capital of the local tribe, the Damnonii, but more excavation is required before such a suggestion could be verified. For a site of that importance the defences are very slight and were the enclosed area smaller it would hardly merit the status of a fort at all. Several other hilltops in Renfrew and north Ayrshire are also occupied by large, poorly defended enclosures and

it is possible that Walls Hill is simply the largest example of a localised type of iron-age (or earlier) enclosure which we have barely begun to understand.

90 Ritchie Ferry, Settlement, Homestead and Enclosure, South Lanarkshire

Later 1st millennium BC—early 1st millennium AD.

NS 945215. From Crawford cross the Clyde and turn left along the minor road that flanks the N side of the river. Follow it for 400 m and park at the W end of the wood. The site lies on an elongated ridge between the valley floor and higher ground to the N.

This inconspicuous ridge was a particularly favoured spot for settlement during the later first millennium BC/early first millennium AD (possibly on account of its sunny aspect and sheltered position), and along its crest there are the remains of no less than three separate settlement sites which show an interesting range of defences and house-types.

The most prominent occupies high ground at the west end of the ridge. This is the largest and most heavily defended of the settlements, but even so, it cannot be classified as a fort, since the single rampart offers only a modest defence, and was built by scraping material from the interior, not by digging an external defensive ditch as would have been the case when building a fort. On the north-west traces of three clearly defined quarry scoops

can be seen cut into the slope behind the rampart. Three of the four gateways lead straight into the interior, but on the south-west anyone entering the settlement would have been turned to the left before climbing up towards the crest of the ridge. In the interior there are the remains of at least eight buildings, all round timber houses but built using two different techniques. The five on the south-west were placed on platforms excavated into the slope and closely resemble the houses seen in unenclosed platform settlements; the second group, which lie in the north-west, are examples of the ring-ditch style, in which the principal posts were set in a continuous bedding-trench, and this trench can still be seen as a slight depression.

The homestead lies to the west of the settlement and is tucked into the foot of the ridge. It comprises

Ritchie Ferry, settlement and homestead

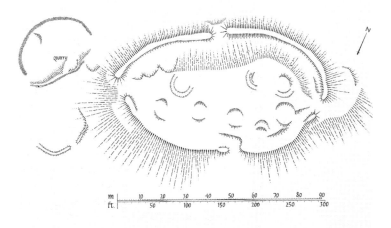

an oval enclosure surrounded by the remains of a ruined stone wall with an entrance on the south-south-west; on the west side of the interior there is a single house platform. To the south-east there are the remains of a small enclosure which may be associated either with the homestead or the settlement. About 75 m east of the settlement there is an embanked enclosure (not illustrated), measuring about 18 m in internal diameter, which may have surrounded a timber house.

The ridge thus contains traces of at least three phases of settlement; without excavation it is not possible to be certain of the chronological relationships between them, but it is likely that the settlement preceded the homestead.

91 Torr a' Chaisteil, Dun, Arran

Late 1st millennium BC—early 1st millennium AD.

NR 922233. From the A 841 follow the signpost (NR 925235) and walk along the track that leads directly to the dun. Parking is difficult, leave the car in Corriecravie or farther to the east.

Historic Scotland.

This dun is typical of the many hundreds of similar small iron-age defensive structures to be found along Scotland's western seaboard. Characteristically, it makes use of a small natural knoll to give added defence but, like many others, it overlooks agricultural land which its occupants would have farmed. Whereas some duns take in the whole summit on which they are built, and are therefore of rather irregular plan, Torr a'Chaisteil was deliberately laid out to be a near true circle measuring 14 m in diameter over a wall up to 3.7 m thick. The wall is now much reduced in height (it may originally have been about 2 m high), but considerable stretches of the outer face can still be seen standing up to two courses high. The entrance is on the east and was protected by an outer bank which crosses the knoll from north to south; such outworks are a common occurrence and give a degree of extra protection to the weakest part of the dun (although it is difficult to imagine that the dun-dwellers were able to withstand anything more than a rather desultory attack). Torr a' Chaisteil has been dug into on at least three occasions, but little additional structural information was recovered and the finds, as is normal on duns, were restricted to the top stone of a rotary quern and the bones of domesticated and wild animals.

Duns of this type were occupied by a single family, who held, and farmed, the surrounding land. The family was almost certainly of noble status and the dun, although it was a defensive structure, was probably built to impress and dominate as much as to function as a stronghold.

Torr a' Chaisteil, Arran, fort

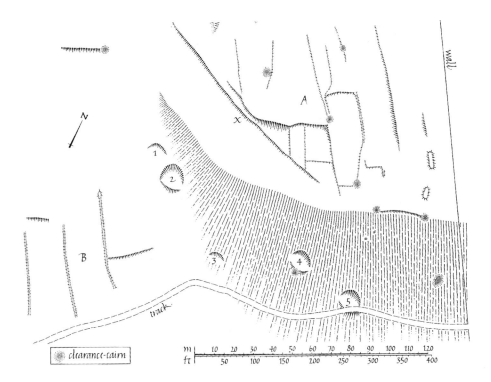

wall

A

X

N

1

2

B

3

4

5

track

m | 10 20 30 40 50 60 70 80 90 100 110 120
ft | 50   100   150   200   250   300   350   400

clearance-cairn

Ellershie Hill, unenclosed platform settlement and field-system

92 Ellershie Hill, Field-system, Unenclosed Platform Settlement and Cairns, South Lanarkshire

2nd to 1st millennium BC.

NS 955194. The easiest approach to Ellershie Hill is to take the Thornhill turning (A 702) off the Carlisle-Glasgow road (A 74), cross the main railway line and park. Then follow a track that begins opposite the first house on the left, after about 100 m take another track that leads to the right and the field-system is situated immediately S of a stone dyke.

In the rough grazing on the south-east flank of Ellershie Hill there is a fragment of a prehistoric landscape containing parts of a field-system, an unenclosed platform settlement and three burial-cairns. Groups of monuments such as this must once have been widespread in Upper Clydesdale, but most have been removed by more recent agriculture, and even at Ellershie the prehistoric field pattern has been encroached on by a later field-system making it impossible to estimate the original extent of the prehistoric settlement.

The prehistoric field-system is divided by a scarp into two sections (A and B on the plan), but the fields are similar in both parts, comprising long narrow enclosures lying at right-angles to the contour and bounded by lynchets or low stony banks. These large strips, or fields, are in many cases subdivided by slight banks into smaller plots. Placed on top of the field-banks, or just inside the fields, there are a number of stony mounds which are probably piles of stones collected from the fields during tilling.

On the scarp between the two sections of the field-system there are five platforms of an unenclosed platform settlement. Two (1 and 3) are poorly preserved but the remainder are clearly visible; no. 5 is cut by the track and on the lip of no. 4 there is a clearance heap. The last element of this cluster of monuments is a group of three cairns situated on the crest of a low ridge to the south of the field-system close to the electricity transmission line, which measures 10 m by 0.6 m, 4.5 m by 0.3 m and 3.4 m by 0.2 m respectively.

The chronological relationships between the various elements of this group are not clear, but it would be simplistic to believe that they are all contemporary, and it is more probable that they represent quite distinct phases of settlement in the vicinity. The burial-cairns are likely to date to the

**Normangill Rig,
unenclosed
platform
settlement**

earlier second millennium, while the unenclosed platforms were built late in the second or early in the first millennium. An approximate date for the field-system is more difficult as so little work has been carried out on them, but somewhere in the iron-age would be appropriate.

93 Normangill Rig, Unenclosed Platform Settlement, South Lanarkshire

Late 2nd—early 1st millennium BC.

**Unenclosed
platform
settlement,
Corbury Hill**

NS 966215. From Crawford take the minor road that leads up the Midlock Water, park about 500 m E of its junction with the Camps Water road and walk up to the E side of a small rectangular plantation which lies over part of the site.

The remains of this cluster of late bronze-age timber houses are the most interesting of a series of similar groups that are concentrated in the valleys of the Camps Water, Midlock Water and Upper Clyde, most of which are to be found within about 30 m of the 300 m contour.

This group consists of five well-preserved platforms which would originally have supported circular timber houses; the largest lies just inside the south-east wall of the wood and is flanked by another two immediately to the east, the remaining two lie slightly lower down the hill. The platforms have been partially levelled into the slope to form an 'eyebrow' at the rear, and the excavated material had been pulled forwards in a semi-circular 'apron' to form a level terrace on which the house was built. The entrances to the houses normally lie at the junction of the eyebrow and apron, and at Normangill they are all situated on the south-east. Although there are many other unenclosed platform settlements in the area this is the only one to be associated with what are probably burial-cairns. These lie on a small shelf immediately to the east-north-east, and comprise about fourteen stony mounds measuring up to 5 m in diameter by 0.7 m in height.

The next group of unenclosed platforms lies only 250 m to the east, just above the public road and by a stone sheep stell. Here, there are at least twelve platforms, and the most interesting feature of this group is the pairing of a large with a much smaller platform; two such pairs form the uppermost four houses of the group. This arrangement of houses suggests some form of functional differentiation, with the larger house possibly serving as a dwelling, while the smaller may have been used as a store.

Before leaving Normangill look south over the Midlock Water and try to spot the group of unenclosed platforms high up on the slope opposite.

PREHISTORIC BURIAL AND RITUAL MONUMENTS

Moss Farm, Machrie, Arran, stone circle no. 6

The remains of burial and ritual sites form the most conspicuous features of the surviving neolithic and bronze-age landscape. Traditionally, the burial sites, ie long, chambered and round cairns, have been separated from the ritual sites, ie henges, stone circles and standing stones, on the basis that they served distinct functions, but it is now generally accepted that such a rigid division obscures the dual nature of many of the sites which combined burial with a wider range of ritual activity.

The earliest of the monuments in this group are the chambered cairns which can be dated at least as early as the fourth millennium BC. Most of those described here belong to the Clyde group, that is they combine a trapezoidal mound, which frequently has a semicircular forecourt at the wider end, with a long slab-built chamber divided into a number of separate compartments by septal slabs.

At some time in the mid third millennium round, non-chambered cairns became the dominent form of burial cairn, and round cairns remained in vogue for at least a millennium. During this period numerous variations on the simple round cairn developed, and the enclosed cremation cemetery (no. 101) is one of the most readily recognizable.

Henges (no. 98), with their characteristic banks and internal ditches, are closely akin to stone circles; both are circular (or near circular) and enclose an area within which ritual activities, including burials, took place. Many excavated henges have shown evidence of circular settings of timber posts which resemble the uprights of stone circles. The group of stone circles at Moss Farm, Arran (no. 96) is one of the most remarkable concentrations of sites in Scotland and is comparable with the cluster of monuments surrounding the great circle at Callanish, Lewis.

Although cup-and-ring markings are frequently associated with standing stones and stone circles, the example chosen for this volume, Ballochmyle (no. 94), has been carved on a rock outcrop. It is one of the most surprising discoveries made in Scottish archaeology in the last decade.

Much has been written in recent years about the extent of prehistoric man's knowledge of astronomy and mathematics. Although it is clear that neolithic and bronze-age men were aware of some of the basic movements of the sun, moon and stars, the degree to which they understood and were able to use this information has probably been greatly exaggerated, as has their command of geometry. Many of the observations cited as evidence of astronomical and mathematical sophistication are open to simpler explanations, and as yet the case must remain not proven.

Ballochmyle, cup-and-ring markings: left rocksheet

Ballochmyle, cup-and-ring markings: right rocksheet

94 Ballochmyle, Cup-and-ring Markings, East Ayrshire

Fourth/third millennium BC.

NS 511251. From the Mauchline to Auchinleck road (A 76) take a minor side road to the south, opposite Ballochmyle Golf Course and 400 m NW of the bridge over the River Ayr. Follow the side road for about 180 m and park on the left by a gate next to a stile. The cliff with the cup-and-ring markings lies on the opposite side of the valley and can be approached for most of the way along a footpath.

This group of late neolithic/early bronze age carvings forms one of the most spectacular in Britain and was only discovered in 1986 when trees in front of the cliff were removed. The cup-and-ring markings are disposed in two principal clusters on a vertical rockface and comprise cups with multiple rings, cups in square 'rings', ringed stars and numerous plain cups. On the left-hand panel as the site is approached from the road, there are also three deer-like carvings and what may be a medieval inscription in Lombardic lettering, as well as a date of 1751, showing that the site was known in the 18th century but had subsequently been lost to view and forgotten.

The carvings, or more correctly, the pecked decoration, have been executed in a number of different styles and show a range of expertise in the competence in the composition of the designs. This suggests that the work was carried out by different carvers, probably over a considerable period, and that the site remained the focus of activity for many generations.

The sandstone on which the carvings have been made is very soft and, unfortunately, the site is prone to vandalism, even rubbing a finger over the markings damages them.

95 Clackmannan Stone, Clackmannan

Late 1st millennium BC—early 1st millennium AD.

NS 911918. In the centre of Clackmannan next to remains of the Tolbooth.

The Clach Mannan (from the Gaelic, Stone of the Manau) is a natural whinstone boulder which, in 1833, was placed on the top of an impressive monolith next to the Tolbooth in Clackmannan. For many years it had been kept in Clackmannan Tower (see no. 40) but it is reputed to have come originally from the foot of Lookaboutye Brae about 1 km to the south (NS 912911).

As the name suggests, the stone is associated with the Manau, a local iron-age tribal group; its precise function, however, is unknown but it may have marked the site of the rallying point for the tribe or indicated a sacred place. The ritual use of a boulder, whether decorated (as are several of the Irish examples) or plain, was not uncommon in the Celtic world, but this practice should not be confused with the much earlier bronze-age tradition of erecting standing stones. Another well-known example can be seen at Lochmaben, Dumfries, where a large natural boulder, the Clockmabon Stone, is associated with the worship of the Celtic god, Maponus. The Manau are also remembered in the placename, Slammanan, which lies on the south side of the Forth.

96 Moss Farm, Machrie, Stone Circles and Cairns, Arran

4th to 2nd millennium BC.

NR 9032. Access to the Moss Farm complex is by foot along a farm track which is signposted from the A 841 about 200 m S of the bridge over the Machrie Water (NR 895330).

Historic Scotland.

The area immediately around the abandoned steading at Moss Farm contains Scotland's most remarkable concentration of neolithic and bronze-age monuments. Included within this group are chambered cairns, round cairns, stone circles, standing stones, and hut-circles and field-systems. Only the principal monuments which are in state care are discussed in detail below, and for the convenience of the visitor the monuments are described from west to east in the order in which they will be encountered if approached from the track to Moss Farm.

1 Cairn (Moss Farm Road)

The track to Moss Farm clips the north side of the sadly mutilated remains of this large round cairn (probably of bronze-age date). It measures about 19 m in diameter and is surrounded by an impressive boulder kerb which, in the past, has led to its erroneous description as a stone circle. The form and size of the cairn are comparable with those of Auchagallon (no. 99) and the two

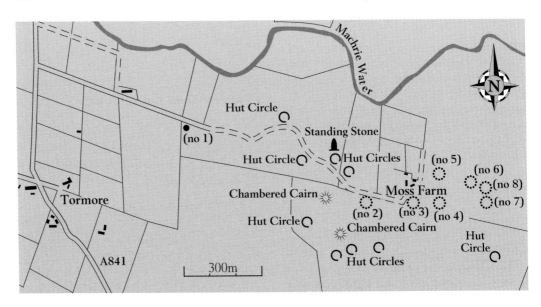

Moss Farm, Machrie, Arran: site plan

monuments are probably closely related. A slit trench which crosses the site is the poorly back-filled remains of a recent excavation.

2 Chambered Cairn

About 110 m south-east of the first gate east of the Moss Farm Road cairn, there are the wasted remains of a chambered cairn which is straddled by the track. Its position is indicated by a lone tree and all that survives are parts of the chamber, lying between the track and the fence, and traces of the mound on the north side of the track.

3 Stone Circle

This unusual stone circle consists of two concentric rings of stones; the outer is slightly egg-shaped and measures about 18 m in maximum diameter, while the inner ring is circular measuring 11.5 m in diameter. The stones of both rings are small rounded boulders and contrast with the impressive slabs seen elsewhere in the complex. Although this site is normally described as a double stone circle, it is not clear if the outer ring was designed as a free-standing setting or was intended to be a kerb to the platform on which the inner circle rests. In the 19th century a cist was discovered in the inner circle.

4 Stone Circle

This small circle now comprises four low granite boulders and it is not known whether there may originally have been more. Excavation in 1861 revealed a central cist containing a Food Vessel, a bronze pin or awl, and a group of flints. The finds are in the National Museums of Scotland, Edinburgh.

5 Stone Circle

Only four of the original total of nine stones of this circle can now be seen and of these three have been reduced to stumps which barely project above the level of the peat. Excavation in 1861 revealed a central cist with a second lying a little to the south. In the latter there was a crouched inhumation accompanied by two flint flakes.

6 Stone Circle

This is the most spectacular of the Moss Farm stone circles with the three surviving uprights standing to a maximum height of up to 5.5 m, making them amongst the tallest standing stones in Scotland. The circle originally consisted of seven or eight stones, and the remains of some of the fallen monoliths litter the surrounding ground. In the more recent past an attempt has been made to reuse one of the fallen stones by converting it to the two halves of a set of mill stones, but the project was abandoned when the upper half broke in two. In 1861 two cists were found in the circle; one contained a Food Vessel with a cremation, and in the second there was a crouched inhumation.

7 Stone Circle

Although several of the stones of this circle (strictly speaking an ellipse) appear to be missing or displaced, it probably originally consisted of a ring of twelve stones arranged in an unusual manner with tall sandstone slabs alternating with squat granite boulders. This is the only circle in the Moss Farm group to have this feature which, in fact, is rarely seen in Scotland as a whole. Recent excavations have shown that the stone circle was preceded by a timber phase with a horseshoe-shaped setting of posts at the centre of the circle.

8 Stone Circle

The preceding stone circles at Moss Farm have all been known since the mid 19th century, but this final circle was only identified recently when attention was drawn to a number of stones projecting through the peat. On excavation they proved to be part of a circle of ten stones, which have subsequently been left exposed. Between the stones there were the post-holes of an earlier ring of timber uprights, indicating a rather more complex history than the surface traces might have suggested.

97 Kinnell, Stone Circle, Stirling

3rd-2nd millennium BC.

NN 577328. From the centre of Killin follow a side-road that runs from the S side of the Dochart Bridge towards Kinnell House.

This small stone circle is situated in a pasture field immediately south-west of Kinnell House. Few circles with stones as tall as these are so well-preserved, and it is possible that the good condition of this example owes more than a little to its proximity to the former home of the MacNab of

MacNab. During the late 18th and early 19th centuries it was fashionable to have antiquities in the parkland surrounding great houses, and the stone circle may have been 'improved' during that period.

There are six stones in the ring and they are arranged on the circumference of a flattened circle measuring 9.5 m by 8.5 m in diameter. Unlike some other circles, the stones are not graded in height but the two tallest stones (up to 2 m high) lie adjacent to each other on the south-west quadrant and they are flanked on the north and east by the two shortest stones (1.2 m high). On the top of the northernmost stone there are three plain cup-marks: this is a rather unusual place to find them as they are normally to be seen on the flat faces of standing stones.

The Kinnell circle is one of the more westerly examples of a large number of stone circles to be found in Perthshire.

----

98 Normangill, Henge, South Lanarkshire

3rd millennium BC.

NS 972221. This site lies in the valley of the Camps Water about 150 m E of the road to Normangill farmhouse and is cut in two by the public road.

Unfortunately, this classic later neolithic ritual monument was not discovered until after the track of the railway (now the public road) had been

driven through its centre; nevertheless it remains one of Scotland's best examples of a henge. It consists of an oval enclosure measuring 40 m by 35 m within a ditch 4 m across and up to 0.3 m deep, which is separated from its accompanying bank by a wide berm. The opposing entrances, which are unusually broad, lie on the north-north-west and south-south-east respectively. Originally, there may have been a setting of large timber posts placed close to the lip of the ditch, leaving an open area at the centre where the rituals would have been performed. On the south-west a recent turf sheepfold has been built over the terminal of the west bank.

----

99 Auchagallon, Cairn, Arran

3rd-2nd millennium BC.

NR 893346. Take the minor road that links the A 841 (Blackwater Foot—Lochranza road) and the B 880 (The String) and park at the foot of the track to Auchagallon farm, close to the signpost. Walk up the track for about 150 m and the cairn is on the right.

Historic Scotland.

The interpretation of this monument is somewhat problematical: it is frequently described as a stone circle, but is more likely to be a localised type of cairn dating from the second or third millennium BC. At present the site consists of a low mound of stones about 13.5 m in diameter surrounded by an intermittent ring of boulders. These are graded in height with the smaller stones lying on the east and five particularly large stones set on the west, close to the track. 19th century records show that the interior has been disturbed and that at one time it was clearer of stones than it is today.

Without excavation it is impossible to disentangle the complex histories of sites such as Auchagallon, and it is all too easy to try to pigeon-hole them into existing schemes of classification. The wide range in the heights of the stones of the ring indicates that it is not a true stone circle in the normally accepted sense, and on balance, the grading of the stones, their intermittent spacing and the presence of a mound suggests that the site is a cairn dating to the late neolithic or early bronze age. For another example of this Arran type of cairn see Moss Farm Road (no. 96,1).

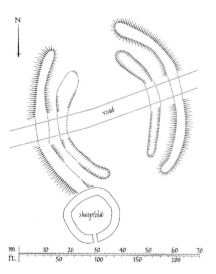

Normangill Henge

**Auchagallon,
Arran: cairn**

Aerial view (Left)

100 Fairy Knowe, Hill of Airthrey, Cairn, Stirling

Late 3rd-early 2nd millennium BC.

NS 796981. The cairn lies on Bridge of Allan golf course. Ask at the club house (NS 792983) for permission to visit.

The Fairy Knowe is a large bronze-age round cairn measuring 18 m in diameter by 2.2 m in height. What distinguishes it from the comparatively sizeable number of similar cairns to be found close by is that it was partly excavated in 1868 and, instead of being totally removed thereafter, was restored and preserved. Such enlightened action frequently occured on large estates where landowners appreciated antiquities as landscape features and did not feel financially constrained to squeeze every available inch for agricultural use. By modern standards the 19th century excavation was technically rather crude and on a limited scale; nevertheless, it tells us a great deal about the date and use of the cairn. A 12 ft (3.64 m) wide trench was driven through the centre of the mound revealing two burial deposits; one was a cist found at the centre, and the other lay high up in the body of the cairn. The central cist was built on top of the old land surface (not dug through it as is often the case), and during construction its end and side-slabs had been supported by a ring of small stones. The floor was formed by a single large slab on which there were the remains of an inhumation together with fragments of charcoal. Once the cist had been sealed, it was covered by a capping of stones, thus creating a small cairn. The rest of the material was then piled over the top of this cairn. Mixed in with the matrix of the mound there were quantities of charcoal, pottery and bones; this is frequently encountered in cairns, and is normally interpreted as the scraped-up debris of feasting rituals associated with the funerary rites of the dead. The other burial was indicated by a Beaker found high up in the cairn. It was clearly a secondary deposit and may have been one of many later burials inserted into the mound.

The excavation showed that the cairn was erected in the early bronze age and was used as a mausoleum, possibly over a long period of time.

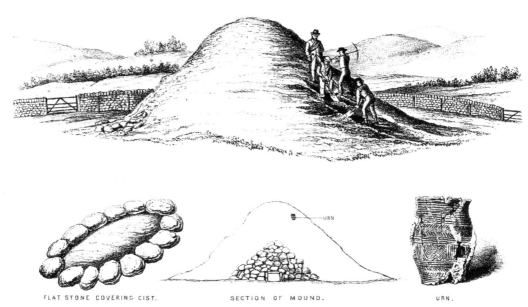

Fairy Knowe, Hill of Airthrey, cairn: nineteenth century excavations

FLAT STONE COVERING CIST. SECTION OF MOUND. URN.

Cairn (Right)

101 Fall Hill, Enclosed Cremation Cemetery, South Lanarkshire

2nd millennium BC.

NS 963217. This site may be approached either by parking at the foot of Fall Hill on the Camps Water Road and walking around the summit of the hill to the coll on the E, or by walking from the unenclosed platform settlement at Normangill Rig (no. 93).

The enclosed cremation cemetery on Fall Hill is the only example of this type of monument to be positively identified in Lanarkshire, and it lies immediately east of the bottom of the coll between Fall Hill and Normangill Rig. It consists of a low circular bank surrounding a small cairn-like mound; the enclosure measures 16 m in diameter within a stony bank which varies from 2.1 m to 3.4 m in thickness but only 0.3 m in maximum height. An unusual feature visible in the bank, and one not seen at any other enclosed cremation cemetery, is a pair of shallow grooves, 0.6 m to 0.8 m apart, which are now discontinuous but originally they probably formed a complete circuit. Although without excavation it is not possible to be certain of their function, it is likely that they supported upright timbers or a wattle screen. Within the enclosure, and lying a little to the north-east of the true centre, there is a grass-grown stony mound 4.3 m in diameter and 0.4 m in height.

Excavation has shown that these monuments are a specialised type of burial-site dating to the bronze age. Only a small number have been found in Scotland, but this is hardly surprising as they are easily confused with hut-circles (particularly where the central mound is small or absent) and, being of rather slight construction, they are prone to destruction.

The burial rite, as the name suggests, is by cremation with the comminuted bones being placed in shallow pits which are normally clustered around the centre of the enclosure and, in many cases, covered by a roughly built cairn or capping of stone. The cremations are rarely accompanied by any gravegoods, which made dating difficult before the discovery of radiocarbon dating methods, but radiocarbon assays from sites at Weird Law, Peebles and Whitestanes Moor, Dumfries have produced dates of about 1700 BC and about 1660 BC respectively.

6 m in height. It is a prominent local landmark, being visible for many miles and, on a clear day, the stiffish walk to the summit is more than handsomely repaid by the magnificent view to be gained of the valley of the Clyde and the Southern Uplands.

Tinto Hill, cairn

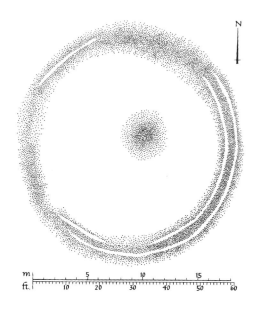

102 Tinto Hill, Cairn, South Lanarkshire

Late 3rd—early 2nd millennium BC.

NS 953343. The public footpath to the top of Tinto Hill begins at Fallburn (NS 964394) (see also no. 88).

The cairn on the summit of Tinto Hill (712 m OD) is one of the largest bronze-age round cairns in Scotland, measuring 43 m in diameter by almost

103 Carn Ban, Chambered Cairn, Arran

4th millennium BC.

NR 991262. Access to this remote cairn is difficult; visitors should walk from the A 841 up the Forestry Commission road to Auchdreoch, then follow the Forest Walk directions to the cairn.

Historic Scotland.

This trapezoidal Clyde-type chambered cairn is situated on sloping ground at a height of about 275 m. Its location in so remote a spot is unusual for the chambered cairns of Arran, as the majority are found close to arable ground, but its very remoteness has helped to preserve it from the depredations of stone robbers, and it remains one of Arran's best-preserved neolithic cairns.

Fall Hill, enclosed cremation cemetery (Left)

The cairn, which is aligned north-east/south-west, measures about 30 m by 18 m and 4.5 m in greatest height; at the north-east end there is a semi-circular forecourt flanked by two square-ended 'horns' projecting from the main body of the mound. At the centre of the forecourt a pair of portal stones marks the entrance to a chamber, which, before excavation in the late 19th century, still remained intact—Carn Ban was the only neolithic cairn on

Arran to retain its roofed chamber. Unfortunately, the roofing lintels have now collapsed, although one can still be seen lying nearby, but the chamber was about 5.6 m long with four compartments, each separated by a septal slab, and it stood to the considerable height of 2.74 m.

At the centre of the south-west end of the cairn, and in line with the main chamber, there are several stones which probably indicate the position of a second chamber. Such additional chambers are comparatively common features in chambered cairns, and either they are inserted to accommodate secondary burials, or they mark an earlier phase in the development of the cairn in which a primary mound (with its chamber) has been incorporated into a greatly expanded cairn. At Carn Ban there is no evidence to suggest which

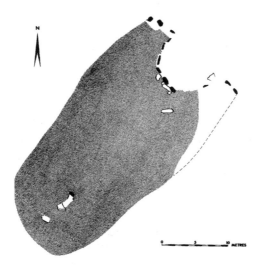

Carn Ban, Arran, chambered cairn

East Bennan, Arran, chambered cairn (Below)

is the case, and only a properly controlled excavation will be able to reveal the answer.

In terms of finds, the 19th century excavations were rather disappointing; the only objects recovered were two flakes, one of Arran pitchstone and the other of flint. The acid soil conditions had reduced any skeletons present to a single fragment of a long bone and a burnt piece of possibly human bone.

104 East Bennan, Chambered Cairn, Arran

4th millennium BC.

NR 993207. From the A 841 (Blackwater Foot— Whiting Bay road) take the track signposted Hillhead and walk across the fields to the cairn.

East Bennan is the classic example of the trapezoidal and horned long cairn of Clyde-type. It measures about 34 m from east to west by 6.7 m at the narrow east end and 19.8 m at the wider west end, but it has been extensively robbed of stone and only stands to a height of 0.9 m. The sides of the mound were revetted by a kerb of boulders, a few of which are still visible. At the west end there is a semicircular forecourt, flanked by square-ended horns, and the remains of an orthostatic (upright stones) facade. At the centre of the facade the two tallest stones act as portals on either side of the entrance to the chamber. However, as they are only 0.15 m apart at ground level, it is difficult to see how this gap functioned as an entrance; it is possible that they are a late addition to the cairn and were inserted during the ritual blocking of the cairn once burials had ceased (cf Monamore, no. 105). The portal stones appear to be deeply buried, and this probably indicates that the forecourt is packed with a considerable depth of blocking material. The chamber is one of the longest in the Arran neolithic cairns and consists of five overlapping pairs of stones, making five compartments which are divided by septal slabs. Like many of the Arran chambered cairns, the chamber was excavated by T H Bryce (in 1909), but it had been cleared out before Bryce's day and all he found was a flake of Arran pitchstone and fragments of a round based pot. At the east end of the cairn there are at least two lateral chambers set at right angles to the long axis of the mound; their relationship to the cairn is uncertain and excavation would be required to tell whether they are part of an earlier cairn incorporated into the later long cairn or secondary chambers inserted after the construction of the primary west chamber.

105 Monamore, Chambered Cairn, Arran

4th to 3rd millennium BC.

NS 017288. Take the Ross road and 400 m W of its junction with the A 841 there is a Forestry Commission carpark (NS 014297). From here take the track that leads uphill and follow the signs for Meallack's Grave.

Forestry Commission.

This cairn is of particular interest as it is the only neolithic tomb on Arran to have been excavated in recent times and, although not especially well-preserved, it is still worth walking through the forest to visit such a classic site. Much of the mound has been removed, but it is trapezoidal on plan measuring about 13.5 m from north-east to south-west by a maximum of 10.5 m at the south-west end. The most prominent features visible today are the three-compartment chamber and some of the stones of the facade which lie at the south-west end of the cairn. Unlike the other Clyde-type long cairns at Carn Ban (no. 103) and East Bennan (no. 104), the forecourt is rather shallow and unsymmetrical, but the facade is well-built with panels of drystone walling (now buried) between the orthostats (uprights). These are roughly graded in height with the tallest standing at the centre, and the middle pair also form portal stones on either side of the entrance to the chamber. The side-slabs of the chamber are set in the characteristic overlapping plan with the compartments divided by septal slabs. At the entrance to the chamber there is a second pair of portal stones placed behind the facade stones and behind them there was a sill-stone, which was probably necessary to prevent soil creeping into the chamber. Bryce cleared out the chamber in 1901 but the only finds were a few tiny fragments of pottery and several chips of Arran pitchstone.

In 1961 Euan MacKie carried out further excavation on the cairn, this time concentrating on the forecourt. Here he found evidence for activity during the period of the cairn's use, comprising fires and 'occupation material' which is normally interpreted as the remains of ritual fires and feasting associated with the cult of the dead. Radiocarbon assays from the bottom and top of this material gave dates of about 3950 BC and 2940 BC respectively which, taken crudely, give a span of use of the cairn of about a millennium. It is, however, difficult to be certain of the true significance of these dates but we can be sure that cairns of this type could have remained in use over a long period. Once the community who built the cairn decided that no more burials were to take place, the forecourt (where all the important rituals had occurred) and the entrance to the chamber were deliberately blocked and filled in with earth and stone, thus sealing the cairn.

106 Torrylin, Chambered Cairn, Arran

4th-3rd millennium BC.

NR 955211. Park by the shop at Torrylin and follow the signpost along the track that leads directly to the cairn.

Historic Scotland.

Stone-robbing has severely reduced the mound of this cairn and it is difficult to be certain of its original shape. The form of the chamber, however, suggests that it is a Clyde-type cairn and the mound was therefore probably rectangular or trapezoidal

Torrylin, Arran, chambered cairn

Torrylin, Arran, chambered cairn

on plan. The best-surviving feature of the cairn is a portion of the chamber, which is aligned north-north-west/south-south-east (probably parallel to the long axis of the cairn). The outer, or entrance, section of the chamber has been destroyed, but parts of at least four compartments are visible. These are built in the characteristic form of Clyde cairns with pairs of large slabs along the long axis of each compartment which overlap the inner end of the slabs of the next chamber. This technique was probably designed to give the side-walls of the chamber greater strength in order to support the considerable weight of the corbelled and lintelled roof. The individual compartments are separated by transverse, or septal, slabs which not only serve to divide up the chamber but, being wedged against the side-slabs of the compartment, also helped to give structural support to the side walls.

Although the cairn has been excavated, or more accurately dug into, on at least three occasions (c 1861, 1896 and 1900), attention has only been paid to the chambers and there is little information about the cairn as a whole. The finds, however, are of some interest and include four human skulls from the third chamber and the remains of at least six adults, one child and an infant from the fourth. Besides the human remains, there was a fragmentary neolithic lugged bowl (now in the National Museum of Antiquities of Scotland in Edinburgh) and a fine flint knife, as well as the bones of domesticated and wild animals (ox, pig, lamb or kid, bird, fish, otter and fox). The domesticated animal bones probably represent the remains of ritual feasts but the otter and fox maybe the remains of animals who used the tomb as a den.

The bones of exotic mammals and birds have been found in other neolithic tombs and the animals may have played a part in the ritual life of these communities.

107 Kilpatrick, Arran

? Neolithic or bronze age.

NR 906262. The track to the site at Kilpatrick is signposted from the main road (A 841) in Kilpatrick.

Historic Scotland.

For many years this site was thought to be a 'cashel' (here used to described an Irish form of Early Christian monastery) and, despite excavation in 1909 by J A Balfour, this interpretation was accepted until comparatively recently. A re-analysis of the field remains, however, suggests that Balfour was mistaken, but there is still no general agreement as to the precise nature of the site.

The remains comprise a large enclosure of a little under one hectare which is surrounded by an earth-and-stone bank, and attached to its north side there is a smaller circular structure. Balfour interpreted the larger enclosure bank as the 'vallum' of the monastery, and the circular structure as the meeting hall of the monks; he also noted three 'monks cells' outside the enclosure to the west. We can now be fairly certain that the 'vallum' is a comparatively recent field-bank with the rig-and-furrow strips it enclosed still visible, and that the three monk's cells to the west are the sites of prehistoric timber houses. The interpretation of the smaller circular structure remains in doubt; it is not monastic in origin, but there is not clear evidence of its function. One suggestion is that it is an iron-age dun, and its hilltop position would favour this, but the discovery during the 1909 excavations of a cist and Food Vessel in the wall, might point to a much earlier date and quite different function. Its position would be in keeping with it being a chambered tomb or bronze-age cairn, and the large slabs still visible in the interior, taken together with the so-called entrance-passage, might suggest that it could easily be a chambered cairn reused in the bronze age. Only excavation can solve the problem and it remains an interesting example of the changing nature and development of archaeological interpretation.

MUSEUMS

MAJOR MUSEUMS

This list of museums is not intended as an exhaustive guide to all the museums in the area covered by this book, but it is designed to draw the visitor's attention to the more important collections of material that complement the field monuments.

EDINBURGH

National Museums of Scotland, Scotland's foremost collection of prehistoric, Roman and later antiquities.

GLASGOW

Art Gallery and Museum, Kelvingrove, has collections of archaeological material from the West of Scotland.

Hunterian Museum, University of Glasgow, contains collections of prehistoric and Roman (particularly from the Antonine Wall) material.

LOCAL AND SPECIALIST MUSEUMS

ARRAN

Isle of Arran Heritage Museum, Roseburn, Brodick. Displays illustrating life on Arran from the prehistoric period to recent times.

BIGGAR

Gladstone Court Museum has reconstructions of life in Biggar in the 18th and 19th centuries.

Greenhill Covenanter's House. A restored 17th-century house.

BO'NESS

Kinneil Museum (see no. 26) has collections of Roman material and displays of local industrial history.

FALKIRK

Falkirk Museum, 15 Orchard Street. Displays of local prehistoric, Roman and later material.

GRANGEMOUTH

Grangemouth Museum, Public Library, Bo'ness Road. Displays illustrating the history of the town and the Forth and Clyde Canal.

KILMARNOCK

Dick Institute, Elmbank Avenue. Collections of local prehistoric material.

KIRKINTILLOCK

Auld Kirk Museum has displays of Roman material from the Antonine Wall.

NEW LANARK

Counting House (see no.7). Displays illustrating the history of New Lanark.

STIRLING

The Smith Art Gallery and Museum, Albert Road. Collections of prehistoric, Roman and later material.

BIBLIOGRAPHY

Breeze, DJ *The Northern Frontiers of Roman Britain*, London, 1982.

Burl, A *The Stone Circles of the British Isles*, London, 1976.

Butt, J The Industrial Archaeology of Scotland, Newton Abbot, 1967.

Cruden, S *Scottish Castles*, London, 1981.

Cruden, S *Scottish Medival Churches*, Edinburgh, 1986.

Dunbar, JG *The Historic Architecture of Scotland*, London, 1966; revised edition 1978.

Fawcett, R *Scottish Medieval Churches*, Edinburgh, 1985.

Fawcett, R *Scottish Abbeys and Priories*, London, 1994.

Fawcett, R *Scottish Architecture: from the accession of the Stewarts to the Reformation 1371-1560*, Edinburgh, 1994.

Hanson, W and Maxwell, GS *Rome's North West Frontier*, Edinburgh, 1983.

Henshall, AS *The Chambered Tombs of Scotland*, vol 2, Edinburgh, 1972.

Hume, JR *The Industrial Archaeology of Scotland 1. The Lowlands and Borders*, London, 1976.

Ordnance Survey *The Antonine Wall*, Southampton, 1969.

McWilliam, C *Scottish Townscape*, London, 1975.

Maxwell, GS *The Romans in Scotland*, Edinburgh, 1989.

Prentice, R *The National Trust for Scotland Guide*, London, 1976.

Ritchie, A (ed) *Govan and it's Early Medieval Sculpture*, Stroud, 1994.

Ritchie, A and Breeze, D J *Invaders of Scotland*, Edinburgh, 1991.

Ritchie, G and A *Scotland: Archaeology and Early History*, Edinburgh, 1991.

Robertson, AS *The Antonine Wall*, Glasgow, revised edition 1990.

Royal Commission on the Ancient and Historical Monuments of Scotland. Inventories have been published for the following areas included in this volume: *Clackmannan*, 1993; *Lanarkshire*, 1978; *Stirling*, 1963; *West Lothian*, 1929.

Brief descriptive lists in the Archaeological Sites and Monuments Series have been issued for the following areas: *Clackmannan and Falkirk Districts*, 1978; *Cumbernauld , Kilsyth and Strathkelvin Districts*, 1978; *Dumbarton, Clydebank, Bearsden and Milngavie Districts*, 1978; *Stirling District*, 1979; *South Kyle and Carrick*, 1981; *North Kyle and Carrick*, 1983.

Royal Incorporation of Architects in Scotland. A most useful series of architectural guides including *The South Clyde Estuary*, 1986; *Clackmannan and the Ochils*, 1987; *Central Glasgow*, 1993; *The North Clyde Estuary*, 1992; *Ayrshire and Arran*, 1992.

Tabraham, C *Scottish Castles and Fortifications*, Edinburgh, 1986.

Thomas, C *Britain and Ireland in Early Christian Times AD 400-800*, London, 1971.

Williamson, E, Riches, A and Higgs, M *The Buildings of Scotland: Glasgow*, London, 1990.

INDEX OF PLACES

Printed in Scotland for HMSO by (3808)
Dd 0293087 C50 10/95